BRITISH RAILWAYS

PAST and PRESENT

No 31

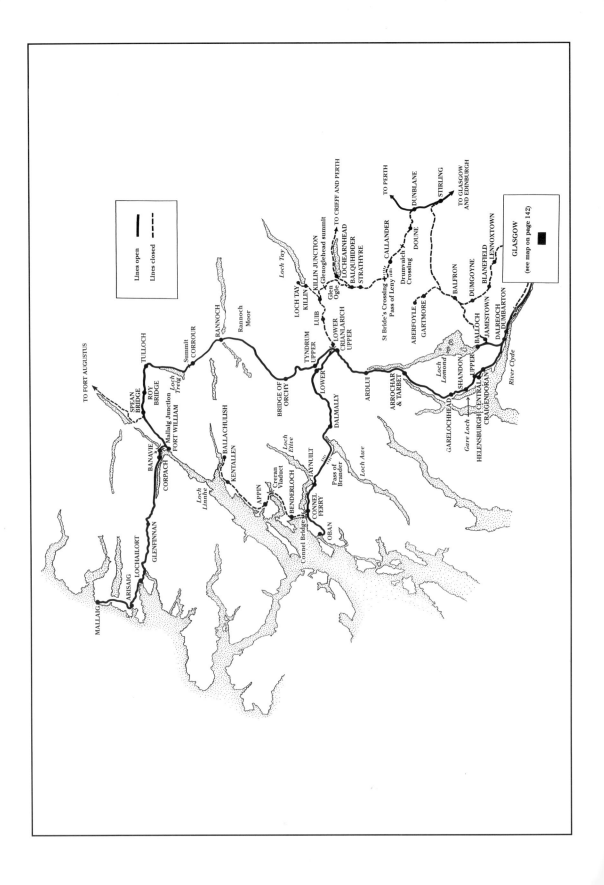

BRITISH RAILWAYS

PAST and PRESENT

No 31

North West Scotland

Keith Sanders & Douglas Hodgins

Past and Present

Past & Present Publishing Ltd

First published in 1998
Reprinted 2001

British Library Cataloguing in Publication Data

A catalogue record for this book is available from the British Library.

ISBN 1 85895 090 2

Past & Present Publishing Ltd
The Trundle
Ringstead Road
Great Addington
Kettering
Northants
NN14 4BW

Tel/Fax: 01536 330588
email: sales@nostalgiacollection.com
Website: www.nostalgiacollection.com

NOTE: All the 'present' photographs have been taken by Keith Sanders; the picture credits refer to the photographers of the 'past' views. All research and captions are by Douglas Hodgins.

Maps drawn by Christina Siviter

Printed and bound in Great Britain

BIBLIOGRAPHY

BR Steam Motive Power Depots, Scottish Region *by Paul Bolger*
An Illustrated History of Glasgow's Railways *by W. A. C. Smith & P. Anderson*
Railway World Special – The West Highland Line *by Neil Caplan*
The West Highland Railway *by John Thomas*

A Regional History of the Railways of Great Britain – Scotland, The Lowlands and the Borders *by John Thomas*
Rails to the Isles *by Bob Avery*
The West Highland Mallaig Extension in BR Days *by Tom Noble*

Additional research kindly supplied by W. A. C. Smith.

BEINN ODHAR: One of the classic railway locations in the United Kingdom, which is still popular to this day. On 12 May 1962 the 3.00pm Fort William to Glasgow (Queen Street) climbs along the flank of Beinn Odhar behind BRC&W No D5360 and 'B1' 4-6-0 No 61352. The distinctive shape of Beinn Dorain (3,524 feet high) can be seen in the background, with the remains of winter snow still visible. The line runs across the base of Beinn Dorain into the Horseshoe Curve (which is hidden from view at this location) and on to the flank of Beinn Odhar as seen. In

CONTENTS

a further 300 yards the train will reach the end of its climb at County March Summit (1,024 feet above sea level). The summit also forms the regional boundary between Strathclyde Region and Central Region. *W. S. Sellar*
   The view on 12 September 1996 shows two Class 37 locomotives, Nos 37170 and 37409 *Loch Awe*, double-heading the 10.30 Fort William yard to Mossend yard freight. The pathway between the camera and the railway is part of the West Highland Way, which in recent years has become a popular route for walkers.

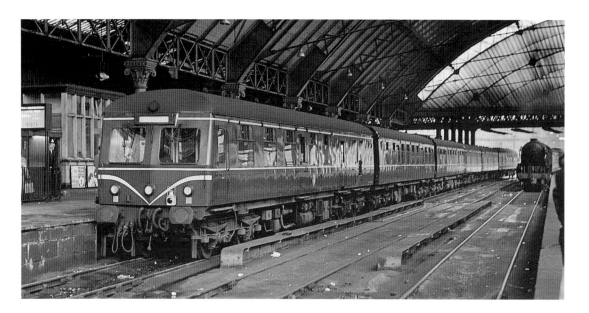

GLASGOW QUEEN STREET: This 13 May 1961 view of platforms 2 and 3 at Queen Street (High Level) shows the 12.10pm to Edinburgh Waverley standing in platform 2 and made up of a Swindon three-car DMU nearest the camera and a Derby three-car unit at the Edinburgh end. Entering platform 3 is 'A2' 'Pacific' No 60530 *Sayajirao* with a parcels train from Edinburgh. Above the DMU can be seen the ornate tops of some of the 48 pillars that supported the overall roof.

Earlier the same day 'N15' 0-6-2T No 69163 stands at the buffer stops waiting to bank the 'Queen of Scots' Pullman out of the station and up Cowlairs incline. The locos used on banking duty were fitted with a wire that ran from the front coupling to the cab via a small pulley set on the smokebox. When the train reached the top of Cowlairs bank a lever in the cab was pulled and the wire lifted the coupling, thus disengaging the banker from

INTRODUCTION

At last, the North West Scotland volume in the 'British Railways Past and Present' series – and undoubtedly the most scenic area of Scotland's railways. Most of this scenery is represented by 'the Highlands' to the north of the area. However, the area covered also includes four city termini, a suburban system and heavy industry, so there is plenty of variety.

The two key players in developing the railways were the Caledonian Railway and the North British Railway. Each had their 'glamour' routes as far as the railway enthusiast is concerned: the Caley built the Callander & Oban line and the NB built the West Highland Line and the Mallaig Extension. Also they both competed for traffic in the north Clydeside area, but with the rationalisation of the 1960s it was usually the Caley lines that closed, leaving the NB lines to survive to this day.

the train. The original method involved hauling the trains up the steep incline by a wire rope and this system lasted for almost 70 years. The introduction of banking locos meant that every departure left the station enveloped in smoke as the 'N15s' performed their duty with gusto. This gave the station a very dirty appearance in steam days. *Both Michael Mensing*

The modern scene has unit No 158727 at the buffer stops on 30 March 1997. Unfortunately the ornate columns have been boxed in, but the glass in the overall roof has been cleaned, giving a much brighter appearance. This is spoiled somewhat by the amount of litter on the track. The platforms have been rebuilt resulting in no centre road between platforms 2 and 3.

The saddest closure must be that of the Dunblane to Crianlarich Lower section of the Callander & Oban line; the sight and sound of steam locomotives pounding up Glenogle must have been quite exhilarating. By way of contrast, it is amazing that the Ballachulish branch survived as long as it did, as the area it served was sparsely populated and could not have generated much traffic. This line was also the most difficult to cover in obtaining the 'present' pictures, as nature has almost completely taken over in the 30 years since closure. The Scottish sapling certainly thrives in the conditions there!

One positive discovery was the condition of the West Highland line station buildings. Even though most of them are no longer in use, they are generally in a good state of repair and nicely painted. Freight traffic is on the increase so the line should be secure for a number of years.

One major success story must be the steam operation on the Fort William to Mallaig line. This was introduced in 1984 as an experiment and has run every summer since. Things looked a trifle uncertain in the mid-1990s, but since a private company has taken over with the support of the local councils and tourist board, it has been properly marketed and goes from strength to strength.

Finally, the usual list of thanks to people without whose help this book would not have been possible: to the photographers who supplied the 'past' pictures, to the landowners who granted permission to go on their property to obtain the 'present' pictures – and often gave some interesting anecdotes – to my co-author for his research and Bill Smith for additional information, to Donald Cameron for the loan of old maps, to Douglas Hume for taking me to some of the more obscure locations around Glasgow and Clydeside, and last but not least to my wife Barbara for putting up with my absences while away with the camera and for proof-reading the manuscript.

Keith Sanders
Longniddry

The Trossachs

ABERFOYLE: Class 'J36' 0-6-0 No 65315 prepares to leave Aberfoyle and return a Stephenson Locomotive Society (SLS) excursion back to Glasgow on 3 May 1958. As can be seen, the station yard was a spacious affair, no doubt to cope with the hoped-for traffic that unfortunately did not materialise. The railway came to Aberfoyle on 1 August 1882 and, being the 'Gateway to the Trossachs', it became a popular destination for many Glaswegians. *W. S. Sellar*

By 5 April 1996 the station site is a large car park. Much new building is in evidence but the mountain behind the town, together with the flats on the right, confirm that it is the same location.

GARTMORE: Class 'K2' 2-6-0 No 61788 *Loch Rannoch* at Gartmore station on 16 May 1959 with an excursion returning to Glasgow, complete with an observation coach coupled to the locomotive. The tour was organised by the Glasgow University Department of Extra Mural Studies. The station was over a mile to the north-east of Gartmore village. *W. S. Sellar*

The site today is a mass of bushes and scrub, with all signs of the railway obliterated by nature. During the 37 years between the two pictures the A81 road has been realigned and now crosses the old trackbed on a new bridge behind the photographer. With the lifting of the railway the bridge in the past picture has been removed and the space infilled to form an embankment.

BALFRON: This view of the station, crossing and signal box was taken on 3 May 1958, and passengers and locals are showing great interest in the same SLS special from Aberfoyle returning to Glasgow (Queen Street). Note the large station house and the tall semaphore signals. *W. S. Sellar*

The view on 5 April 1996 shows that the station house has been demolished and the railway and level crossing are long since gone. To the left, out of shot, stands a modern residence complete with paddock and stables, the latter being located where the right-hand platform stood. The bridge in the background still remains as it carries Glasgow's water supply in large pipes.

DUMGOYNE: In its early days the station was called Killearn, but it was so far from the village of that name (2 miles) that it was renamed Dumgoyne. With the last passenger train having run on 29 September 1951, it is small wonder that so many people turned out on 3 May 1958 to witness the SLS special to Aberfoyle hauled by 'J36' No 65315. The train has paused at the station for a photo stop. *W. S. Sellar*

By 5 April 1996 there is no sign of any railway station or track. The building that stood to the left of the station, The Beech Tree Inn, still remains and is a very pleasant hostelry that serves excellent food. The trackbed is now part of the West Highland Way and the inn derives much business from passing walkers. In addition, Dumgoyne Distillery is open to visitors and well worth a visit!

BLANEFIELD: 'K2' 2-6-0 No 61788 *Loch Rannoch* pauses at Blanefield station with the Glasgow University railtour to Aberfoyle on 16 May 1959. The station building can be seen on the right, but the foreground area has a decidedly unkempt appearance. *W. S. Sellar*

The view on 5 April 1996 shows that the whole site has gone back to nature, with nothing to indicate that a railway ever passed through.

LENNOXTOWN: Another view of the Glasgow University railtour. Behind the sparkling 'K2' were two Gresley-designed panelled coaches and the observation coach. *W. S. Sellar*

The railway at Lennoxtown closed on 4 April 1966, and 30 years on the station site is now part of a playing field, all railway evidence having been swept away.

JAMESTOWN, near Balloch, on the former Forth & Clyde Junction line, is seen here on 11 May 1958; it served a small village with a population of less than a thousand. The Dalmonach Print Works was located nearby and the railway built a siding into the works. The siding crossed a busy main road and this caused the Local Authority to impose stringent conditions on the operating of trains, to protect both pedestrians and road traffic. *W. S. Sellar*

The present picture, taken slightly to the right and from a lower position, shows the scene on 14 September 1996. The lamp-post stands where the tall semaphore was located and the trackbed beyond the former crossing is now the access road to an industrial estate. The buildings surrounding the station in the 'past' picture have all been demolished, as has the signal box and the station itself. Quite a transformation!

Callander & Oban line: Doune to Crianlarich

The Callander & Oban line was completed through to Oban in 1880; the Caledonian Railway began to promote the route and traffic increased rapidly. There was a considerable amount of freight carried, as Oban was a major fishing port; it was also a popular holiday destination for people living in central Scotland, and through carriages from Edinburgh were provided, usually being attached to Glasgow-Oban trains at Stirling. There were also through trains to London Euston, one being a sleeping car service, but over the years the services were gradually reduced until in 1965 there were only three trains a day between Oban and Glasgow, with the sleeper only running to Oban on Friday nights and returning to London on Monday nights.

The rockfall in Glenogle in 1965 caused the closure of the line east of Crianlarich, so since that time all Oban trains have used the West Highland line to Crianlarich, then taken the chord line in order to regain the old Callander & Oban line.

Traffic today consists of Class 156 'Sprinters'. There is no sleeper service and apart from some timber traffic there are no regular freight workings, However, the line does look secure for the time being.

DOUNE (1): On 9 October 1965, some three weeks before closure of the line, Stanier Class '5' 4-6-0 No 45396 enters Doune station with the 1.18pm Callander-Glasgow (Queen Street) train. Today the station site has taken on a rather unkempt appearance and much of the site has been left to nature. *Fred Landery*

DOUNE (2): The 1966 view illustrates the former grandeur of the station buildings, but they have all since been demolished and the site is now used by H. Campbell & Sons, Timber Merchants. In the 8 June 1996 view some of the platform edging slabs are still visible, as is the road overbridge in the background. *Norman Turnbull*

DRUMLOIST ROAD: Between Doune and Callander a road to Drumloist leaves the A84 and immediately crossed over the railway. Preserved ex-CR 'Single' No 123 is seen on an SLS/BLS 'Easter Rambler' railtour on 12 April 1963, about to pass under the bridge. The A84 road crossed under the railway to the rear of the train. *W. S. Sellar*
    On 12 September 1996 the railway has long gone, and the bridge over the A84 road has been removed; motorists on the road today would never realise that a railway had once crossed at that spot.

DRUMVAICH (1): Situated some 4 miles west of Doune was Drumvaich passing loop. On a gloomy 23 May 1964 'V2' 2-6-2 No 60818 heads the 12.00 noon Callander-Stirling local train – super-power for a two-coach train! 'V2' Class locos were not usually allowed on this line, so one can only speculate as to the reason. *W. S. Sellar*

On 26 August 1996 the scene is little changed apart from the absence of the 'railway furniture', although the lineside hut still survives.

DRUMVAICH (2): Looking to the east on 1 February 1964, we see Standard Class '4' 2-6-4T No 80125 approaching Drumvaich Crossing with the 11.10am Stirling to Callander service. The signal box with attached living accommodation was a feature at five locations on the Callander & Oban line. *Douglas Hume*

The buildings were still standing on 8 March 1997, although the former signal box needs some attention. The route of the line is clearly visible beyond the gate.

CALLANDER (1): On 12 April 1963 CR No 123 has arrived from the east with the 'Easter Rambler' railtour. The picture gives a fine view of the impressive station buildings, which all appear to be in first-class order. *W. S. Sellar*
  At the same location on 14 September 1996 the site of the station is now a large coach and car park. The road overbridge (Station Road) and the roof of the house to the left are the linking features.

CALLANDER (2): At the western approach to the station Class '5' 4-6-0 No 45468 arrives with an Oban-Glasgow (Buchanan Street) train. Note the impressive signal box above the third coach and the typical Caledonian lattice signal posts. *David A. Anderson*

The modern-day view shows the tarmac of the car park and trees and bushes on what used to be well-maintained embankments.

CALLANDER (3): This general view of the station looking west from the Station Road bridge depicts an ex-LMS 2-6-4T in the up platform and also shows the extent of the station with avoiding lines and two bay platforms. *W. A. C. Smith*

Callander is now an extremely busy town, especially in the tourist season, hence the extensive coach and car park. What a great pity that no part of the railway exists – a preserved line would probably thrive with the thousands of tourists who come to the area.

PASS OF LENY: 'B1' Class 4-6-0 No 61396 slips to a stand on the climb from Callander to Strathyre. The bridge in the background crossed the river in the Pass of Leny and half a mile beyond that another bridge crossed the Falls of Leny. As can be seen, it is a damp day and the greasy rails have caused the loco to stall. The 'B1' was a rare class on this line, and such a performance would not have endeared it to the crew. *Hugh Ballantyne*

The 8 June 1996 view shows that all trace of the railway has been erased and the trackbed is now used as a car park for walkers climbing up nearby Ben Ledi. The wall at the end of the avenue of trees is built on the bridge abutment, the bowstring bridge having been removed.

ST BRIDE'S CROSSING (1): Class '5' 4-6-0 No 45396 heads a combined Glasgow/Edinburgh to Oban train on 3 July 1957. The location is just north of the Pass of Leny and is typical of the beautiful countryside in these parts. *David A. Anderson*

At the same location on 8 June 1996 the only visible sign of the railway is the embankment, which is slowly being hidden by trees and bushes. The fence in the foreground is still there, but has been renewed and a static caravan resides in the field.

26

ST BRIDE'S CROSSING (2): Stanier Class '5' No 45099 at the head of an Oban to Glasgow (Buchanan Street) train drifts downhill towards St Bride's Crossing and the scenic Pass of Leny. The date is 6 August 1957, and judging by the fields to the rear of the train, haymaking is in full swing. *W. S. Sellar*

The scene on 8 June 1996, taken from a lower level because of tree growth, shows that the railway is but a memory. Static caravans now dot the landscape, but to the north the distinctive shape of Ben Vorlich (985 metres) continues to dominate the scene.

27

Opposite STRATHYRE: A Stanier Class '5' pauses at Strathyre Station on 23 August 1960 with an Oban-bound train. On 8 June 1996 once again it is all change – no trace of the station remains, the site now being occupied by several houses. *Hugh Ballantyne*

This page In the left background of the 'past' view opposite, just in front of the signal box on the up platform can be seen a heron on a plinth. This close-up view was taken on 12 March 1966. *Norman Turnbull*

With the closure of the station the heron found a new home in the front garden of a guest house in the village, and the casting has now been painted.

BALQUHIDDER (1): On 23 April 1961 Stanier Class '5' No 45049 stands at the signal with an Oban-bound freight. The layout was generous to say the least, as it had the status of a junction station. However, this was lost with the closure of the 2 miles of line between Balquhidder and Lochearnhead in October 1951. *Noel Machell*

The present-day scene on 8 June 1996 shows the site in use as a caravan and camping site.

BALQUHIDDER (2): The second day of the year in 1962 was a perfect winter's day with a good covering of snow on the ground. Class '5' No 45158 is seen on the 12.56pm Oban to Glasgow (Buchanan Street) service approaching the station. Judging by the conditions the small snowplough fitted to the locomotive was a wise precaution just in case the weather worsened. *W. S. Sellar*

By 12 April 1997 the trackbed is just a forest of trees. The 'present' picture has been taken further back, and shows the walled-off trackbed where the bridge over the 'old' A82 used to be and which the Class '5' was approaching. The A82 has been realigned some 100 yards to the east at this point.

LOCHEARNHEAD: This view of the station on 12 March 1966 was taken less than a year after closure. The line from Lochearnhead to Balquhidder opened in 1905 and to many this was not a branch off the Callander & Oban line but an extension of the Perth to Crieff line (see 'British Railways Past & Present' No 9, page 93). The line was closed in October 1951 when the last trains ran on the Comrie-Lochearnhead-Balquhidder section. *Norman Turnbull*

Since its closure the station building has provided a base camp for the Hertfordshire Scouts, who have kept the building in good order as can be seen from the June 1996 picture. The only real change has been in the growth of the bushes and trees.

ABOVE LOCHEARNHEAD: The main line climbed from Balquhidder station for 2 miles before entering Glen Ogle. The closure of the line was hastened by a rockfall at the bottom of the Glen, high above the village of Lochearnhead. This picture taken in July 1966, shows the extent of the rockfall, which forced the closure of the line on 28 September 1965; a bus service was provided for a few weeks until 1 November. Some say that the fall was caused deliberately to ensure the closure of the line, and it does seem strange that to this day very few additional rocks have landed on the trackbed in the 30 years since closure. *Norman Turnbull*

GLENOGLE VIADUCT: A Glasgow-bound train threads its way across the viaduct in May 1963 powered by a BRC&W/Sulzer 1,250hp Bo-Bo diesel-electric locomotive. *Norman Turnbull*

At the same spot on 8 June 1996 the railway trackbed is now a well-used walkway. Beyond the viaduct bushes and trees mark the route of the line, but little else has changed. The viaduct parapet does seem to have been strengthened and widened, but the surrounding hills still have a rather barren look about them.

GLEN OGLE: A sunny 17 May 1961 shows North British diesels Nos D6102 and D6123 making steady progress up the south-west side of the Glen with the 12.00 noon Glasgow (Queen Street) to Oban service. There is just a mile to go to the summit. At this time half of the services were diesel-hauled, but the unreliable NB locos were normally used in multiple. *Michael Mensing*

On 8 June 1996 trees and bushes occupy the trackbed and only the road traffic on the north-east flank of the Glen disturbs the peace.

LOCHAN LAIRIG CHEILE: Stanier 4-6-0 No 44794 heads a down goods with only half a mile to go to the summit at Glenoglehead. The photographer admits this was a 'grab shot' on 18 August 1959, but in addition to the train the car is also of interest. *J. C. Beckett*

The only evidence of the railway on 8 June 1996 is the trackbed, on which the cars are parked. The road has been upgraded and is much busier. The loch is all but hidden by the foreground trees, while there is now a forest on the far hillside.

GLENOGLEHEAD: On 12 May 1962 CR No 123 and NBR No 256 *Glen Douglas* pass Glenoglehead Crossing with an SLS special train returning from Oban en route to Dundee. *W. S. Sellar*

Some two years earlier, on 22 August 1960, Stanier 4-6-0 No 45178 is seen entering the loop with a train for Glasgow. *Hugh Ballantyne*

The scene on 8 June 1996 shows that the platforms still survive, as does the station building. The latter has been converted into two private dwellings, the southernmost of which has had a large extension added to the rear. It was half a mile to the north-west of this location that an RAF Tornado crashed into the hillside on 1 September 1994, tragically killing both crew members, Flt Lt Harrison (aged 33) and Flt Lt Mosley (aged 31). A memorial to the pair has been erected in the picnic spot opposite the former station building.

KILLIN JUNCTION (1): Dropping down from Glenoglehead, Class '5' 4-6-0 No 44880 enters Killin Junction station with the 12 noon Glasgow (Buchanan Street) to Oban train on 16 May 1960. Passengers would alight here to join the branch train for the short journey to Killin or Loch Tay. Note the tall semaphore signals to the rear of the train. At this time the station had no road access, the nearest road being some half a mile away to the north. *Michael Mensing*

On 23 June 1996, apart from the platform from which the 'past' photograph was taken, all trace of the railway has gone, with the hill in the left background being the only other recognisable feature.

KILLIN JUNCTION (2): This busy scene depicts ex-CR '2F' 0-6-0 No 57441 standing in the station on 27 April 1961 with a freight from the village of Killin. Judging by the jacket hanging on the lamp-post, the locomotive crew are probably in the station building enjoying a brew! *Noel Machell*

The same location on 23 June 1996 shows a total transformation, with only the platform edge visible. The station buildings, footbridge and telegraph poles are but a memory, with vegetation now gaining the upper hand.

One of only two branches on the Callander & Oban line, the 5-mile-long Killin branch opened on 13 March 1886 and closed to rail traffic on 28 September 1965, following the blockage of the main line by a landslide in Glen Ogle. The official closure date of the branch is given as 1 November 1965; from 28 September until that date the services were provided by buses.

The branch ran to the village of Killin and then on to Loch Tay Pier. Built by the Killin Railway Company, the 1-mile stretch from Killin to Loch Tay was closed to passengers on 11 September 1939, with the outbreak of war, and was never re-instated. However, it still saw daily activity as the shed for the Killin branch locomotive was at Loch Tay.

Opposite KILLIN JUNCTION (3): A view of the branch platform, with the 11.27am to Killin awaiting departure time. The locomotive is ex-CR 0-4-4T No 55263 hauling a single coach. Judging by the open cab door, the crew are having a breather before the short journey commences. *Michael Mensing*

In June 1996 the remains of the platform are still identifiable. Also visible is the gable end of a stone cottage, which was hidden behind the locomotive in the 'past' picture. The former trackbeds are used as forestry roads, the station forming a pleasant clearing within a Forestry Commission plantation.

This page KILLIN: Another look at No 55263 on the branch train, this time standing in Killin station on 22 August 1960. The station building is badly in need of painting and it all adds up to a sombre scene, not helped by the Scottish summer weather. *Hugh Ballantyne*

The hills in the background are the only link with the 'past' picture, as the station site is now a car park.

LUIB (1): One of the few Stanier Class '5s' to carry a name, No 45158 *Glasgow Yeomanry* rolls into Luib station on the evening of 17 May 1961. The train, a combination of the 6.00pm Glasgow (Buchanan Street) and the 5.30pm Edinburgh (Princes Street) to Oban, was one of several that were still steam-hauled at that time. *Michael Mensing*

The present-day scene shows that the trackbed has been infilled between the platform faces and the site is in use as the Glen Dochart Caravan Park, although the platform edging slabs can still be seen in places. The owners of the park, Bryan and Margaret Donaldson, live in the station buildings, which can be seen to the left of the picture.

LUIB (2): Looking west on 26 June 1970, the down platform building still remains nearly four years after the line's closure. *Norman Turnbull*

Today the site is kept very tidy and very few visitors would realise that it was a former railway location.

WEST OF LUIB: This fine study shows Caledonian Railway No 123 on a railtour half a mile after passing Luib station. On that day, 12 April 1963, the passengers experienced weather conditions from all four seasons of the year! *Rodney Lissenden*
By 23 June 1996 only the hill in the background provides the link between the pictures, as a road now occupies the trackbed and trees obscure the view of the River Dochart.

CRIANLARICH LOWER JUNCTION: On 27 May 1965 D5350 is engaged in a shunting movement between Crianlarich Upper and Lower stations. The train is approaching what used to be known as Crianlarich Glasgow Junction, using the chord line from the West Highland line to the Callander & Oban line. The junction was controlled by the signal box in the picture, situated on the Callander & Oban line. In the background is the bridge carrying the West Highland line over the Callander line, and beyond that is Crianlarich Lower station. The chord was opened on 20 December 1897 and the first regular Glasgow to Oban service via the West Highland line and the chord ran on 23 May 1949. Since the closure of the Callander & Oban line east of Crianlarich in 1965 all Oban services have used the West Highland line to Crianlarich Upper, then used the chord. *Noel Machell*

On 19 June 1994 a Class 37 diesel works a 'West Highlander' tour over the chord; the line has been singled and all the pointwork, signals and signal box are things of the past. The former Callander line is now a siding, which was disused until late 1996 when timber began to be loaded at this point to be taken south by rail.

CRIANLARICH LOWER: A study of the Callander & Oban station as it was in May 1964. The platform is afforded some shelter from the elements by the canopy, a necessary requirement in this part of the world. The station closed in September 1965 following the withdrawal of services as a result of the Glenogle rockfall. *Norman Turnbull*

At the site of Crianlarich Lower station on 23 June 1996 all trace of the station has gone, to be replaced by a small housing development. With just two houses completed, work seems to have ceased.

Callander & Oban line: Crianlarich to Oban

TYNDRUM LOWER: The village of Tyndrum is unique in that it is served by two stations, Upper Tyndrum on the West Highland line to Fort William (see page 98) and, half a mile to the west, Tyndrum Lower on the Oban line. The 'past' picture shows Stanier Class '5' No 45367 approaching the Lower station with the 12.00 noon Glasgow (Buchanan Street) to Oban service on 19 May 1960.
Michael Mensing

Yet again it is all change in the 'present' picture, with the station now consisting of only a single platform and track with modern lighting and a 'bus shelter'-type platform building. Owing to the vegetation to the south of the station the 1996 picture was taken from the north end of the station.

Opposite DALMALLY: On 12 May 1962 the station buildings and signal box have a well-kept appearance, and indeed not much seems to have changed with the present scene on 12 September 1996. Appearances can be deceptive, however, for with the introduction of RETB (Radio Electronic Token Block) signalling in December 1987 the signal box is now closed. The station buildings still stand, but the awning is devoid of glass. *Gavin W. Morrison*

This page The August 1985 view of the down platform shows another heron on a plinth, but unlike the heron at Strathyre (see page 29) it has had its beak and legs painted. The visit in September 1996 revealed only the plinth of Cruachan Granite surviving, the cast-iron heron apparently having been smashed off in gales; it is believed to be in the custody of Scotrail.

LOCH AWE: Without doubt, one of the most scenic locations on the Oban line is the Awe bridge that crosses the River Orchy at the head of Loch Awe. On 23 May 1962 CR No 123 pilots NBR No 256 *Glen Douglas* on an enthusiasts' special. *Gavin W. Morrison*

The present-day scene shows little change from that of 30 years ago other than the photographer having to use a narrower angle because of tree growth along the river bank. The 14.33 Crianlarich to Oban service crosses the bridge on 12 September 1996.

PASS OF BRANDER: The 12.00 noon Glasgow (Buchanan Street) to Oban threads its way through the Pass of Brander on 16 May 1960, hauled by Stanier Class '5' 4-6-0 No 44880. The train is approaching a set of automatic signals that form part of a rock-fall protection system. A system of wires on the north side of the line is connected to all the signals in the pass, and if a rock-fall disturbs them the signals return to danger. The system was designed by John Anderson, Secretary of the Callander & Oban Railway; when the wind blows through the wires it causes them to vibrate like piano wires, so the system is affectionately known as 'Anderson's Piano'. *Michael Mensing*

The system still exists but the arms are know upper-quadrant. The exact view could not be replicated as it is not possible to hang out of the windows of 'Sprinters'!

TAYNUILT: Stanier Class '5' No 45214 enters Taynuilt station on 17 May 1960 with a down freight consisting of ten Presflo alumina wagons being conveyed from Burntisland in Fife to Ballachulish for the British Aluminium Co's plant at Kinlochleven. *Michael Mensing*

It is a much changed scene today with vegetation now obscuring much of the landscape. Gone is the well-kept look of the past to be replaced by the rather untidy look of today as Class 156 'Sprinter' No 156449 arrives with the 15.16 to Oban on 25 August 1996. The road bridge in the background survives, as do the railings bordering the path from the station to the road. A small brewery occupied part of the station buildings for a number of years, but even that now seems to be closed.

CONNEL FERRY was the junction station for the Ballachulish branch, and in this busy scene looking east at on 20 May 1960, ex-Caledonian '2P' 0-4-4T No 55238 has propelled its train out of the station, run round the coaches and is seen having drawn back into the same platform. The locomotive crews are changing over as was the regular practice on this working, the 2.57pm Ballachulish to Oban. Sister locomotive No 55224 is at the head of the train on the right. *Michael Mensing*

The 'present' picture, taken on 25 August 1996, shows a dramatic transformation. The two island platforms have gone, giving way to a single platform face, which is more than adequate with no branch to serve. The station is now an unstaffed halt with a 'bus shelter' waiting room, and the trees on the right hide the remains of the southern platform. The Shell Oil Terminal is still rail-connected, but there is no rail traffic at present.

OBAN MOTIVE POWER DEPOT (63D): A sad sight at Oban MPD on 13 May 1961 as four 'Caley' 0-4-4Ts are stored out of use. The locomotives, Nos 55226, 55195, 55230 and 55238, look rather forlorn, while on the extreme left No 55124 is in steam and waiting to enter the shed yard. *Michael Mensing*

The scene today is barely recognisable as vegetation blots out the line below. The Esso Oil Terminal is still rail-connected but has no rail traffic at present. All trace of the Motive Power Depot has gone, together with the sidings and playing fields, which are now buried under a modern industrial complex. The row of tenements that overlooked the sidings remain, as does Oban's famous landmark, McCaig's Folly, on the skyline to the left of the picture.

OBAN (I): '2P' 0-4-4T No 55224 backs empty stock into Oban station on 24 May 1960. The station always had a rather cramped layout, so following an arrival there was usually a fairly complicated shunting movement. *Michael Mensing*

The scene on 26 August 1996 shows a simplified track layout as 'Sprinter' No 156492 arrives. Again vegetation hides many of the common features, but McCaig's Folly continues to dominate the landscape.

59

OBAN (2): A classic scene on 18 May 1960 as ex-Caledonian Railway '2P' 0-4-4T No 55238 draws empty stock out of the station towards the bridge from which the previous photographs were taken. *Michael Mensing*

The comparison view on 26 August 1996 shows that the houses remain, the bridge has been recently painted and the railway is dominated by RETB radio signalling signs with the track layout much simplified. The surrounding vegetation has grown unchecked.

OBAN (3): On 23 August 1960 Stanier Class '5' 4-6-0 No 44881 awaits departure from Oban. An earlier arrival behind another 'Black Five' can be seen in the left-hand platform. The overall roof is clearly visible at the end of the platforms, but in its latter days it was declared unsafe and trains had to start from platforms outside the roofed area. *Hugh Ballantyne*

On 26 August 1996 it is a much changed picture as the station now only has two platform faces; the overall roof and station building have been demolished and in their place a small brick-built station building has been erected beyond the buffer stops.

Callander & Oban line: the Ballachulish branch

This 27-mile-long scenic branch ran from Connel Ferry (6 miles from Oban) to Ballachulish on the shore of Loch Leven. The line opened for business on 21 August 1903 and had no fewer than seven intermediate stations along its length. They were, from south to north, North Connel, Benderloch, Creagan, Appin, Duror, Kentallen and Ballachulish Ferry. Construction of the line took six years, and it was expensive to build, with two notable viaducts, Connel across Loch Etive and the Creran over Loch Creran.

Traffic grew rapidly in the early years, particularly in the summer months as many tourists took advantage of the line to travel to Ballachulish in order to explore nearby Glencoe. At its peak the branch boasted no fewer than five passenger trains each way per day, but latterly the service was reduced to running between Ballachulish and Connel Ferry, where passengers had to alight for connections to Oban or Glasgow. The branch closed on 28 March 1966.

CONNEL BRIDGE: 'Caley' 0-4-4T No 55238 heads the 10.48am Ballachulish to Connel Ferry service off the bridge on 21 May 1960. The bridge was designed along the lines of the Forth rail bridge, and carried both road and rail traffic in its earlier days. *Michael Mensing*

Nowadays only road traffic uses the bridge, which spans Loch Etive, and immediately under the bridge are the Falls of Lora, a spectacular tourist attraction. As it only carries a single carriageway the bridge is controlled by traffic lights and this can lead to lengthy delays in the summer months.

Opposite BENDERLOCH: The oldest surviving 'Caley tank', No 55124, built in 1895, is seen leaving Benderloch station on 19 May 1961 with the 4.55pm Oban to Ballachulish train. *Michael Mensing*

The picture on 26 August 1996 is all too familiar – all the former railway has been obliterated by a screen of bushes and trees. The buildings in the left background of the 'past' picture are just visible, but the tower of St Modan's church is now hidden from view.

CRERAN VIADUCT (1): BRC&W Bo-Bo diesel No D5366 works off the south end of Creran Viaduct (also known as Creagan Bridge) with an Oban train on 12 July 1965. *Michael Mensing*

The present-day photograph, taken on 26 August 1996, shows that this end of the bridge is very overgrown, necessitating a compromise viewpoint. The stonework and main girders of the bridge seem to be in good order with just the decking causing concern.

The third photograph is a general view of the bridge, looking eastwards.

CRERAN VIADUCT (2): No D5352 curves off the north end of the viaduct with a Ballachulish service on the same day. *Michael Mensing*

Again the present-day view has been taken closer to the bridge and to the left because of vegetation and trees obscuring the view from the original position. As can be seen, the trackbed over the bridge has been fenced off as it is unsafe. However, a pedestrian footpath is still available along the east side of the structure. Who knows what the future may hold for the bridge, as like Connel it could be utilised for road traffic, which would remove the need for motorists to go round the head of the loch as at present and thus save 6 miles on their journey.

APPIN station was photographed on a dull 27 August 1965 as D5356 passed through with the daily 12.08pm Ballachulish to Oban freight. This was just seven months before the branch closed. Appin boasted a large station house with a large awning over the platform (hidden by the train). A feature of the house was its concrete construction. *Noel Machell*

As the 'present' picture shows, by 26 August 1996 the house had long been demolished and the site left to nature. The platforms, however, survive, the up one being used by a local contractor for the storage of plastic pipes.

KENTALLEN (1): D5366 trundles into Kentallen station on 12 July 1965 with the 12.35pm Connel Ferry to Ballachulish service. *Michael Mensing*
  The platforms remain intact and have been incorporated into an extension of the Holly Tree Hotel and Restaurant. The extension looks out across Loch Linnhe to the Ardgour area of Lochaber.

KENTALLEN (2): A few moments later D5366 pulls away from the station. The line followed the edge of Lochs Linnhe and Leven until it arrived at Ballachulish, and the views from the train made the branch a particularly scenic line. *Michael Mensing*

Today the trackbed forms a garden area to the hotel and it must be very pleasant to sit here with a cool drink and watch the sunset over the loch at the end of a hot summer's day. It is nice to see that the lamps are in keeping with the site's former use.

BALLACHULISH (1): 'Caley Tank' No 55195, complete with stovepipe chimney, is ready for departure to Connel Ferry. The station building is beyond the buffer stops. *W. A. C. Smith*

The same view in 1996 shows a modern house where the first coach stood, which obscures the station building. The latter has survived and is in use as the Ballachulish Medical Centre, the name carried on a board in the shape of the old BR totem – a nice touch. The quarry face in the background of the main 'past and present' pictures is unmistakeable. Out of sight to the left of the scene is the old motive power depot building, but it is in very poor condition.

BALLACHULISH (2): On 27 August 1965, D5367 arrives at Ballachulish station with the 12.30pm service from Connel Ferry. The semaphore signals, water crane and, behind the first coach, the signal box are all visible.
Noel Machell

By 25 June 1996 only the outline of the background mountain provides the evidence that this is the same location, as the site is now given over to modern bungalows.

North Clydeside

KELVIN HALL (formerly PARTICK CENTRAL): The Scottish Industries Exhibition held at the Kelvin Hall, Glasgow, in 1959 resulted in many special trains being run for the event. Partick Central was renamed Kelvin Hall on 15 June 1959 prior to the exhibition opening, In connection with the exhibition the 'famous four' preserved Scottish Region locos were brought into service and many of the special trains, which ran from all parts of Scotland, were double-headed by two of these locos; the preserved GWR 4-4-0 *City of Truro* was also used. On 9 September 1959 'B1' 4-6-0 No 61108 is seen entering the station with an excursion to the exhibition. The siding at the back of the station served a scrap metal merchant and an oil depot and survived until 1978, only being closed because of work on the Argyle line. The entrance to the station was built on a stone-faced embankment, which rose from the rocky bed of the River Kelvin below. *W. S. Sellar*

As can be seen in the picture taken on 30 January 1997, the embankment and background bridge remain, although the station lost its passenger and goods traffic in 1964 and the track was subsequently removed. The railings and platforms remain, albeit concealed by a mass of bushes. The black building in the centre background remains, but the demolition of other buildings on the right-hand side now reveals the roof of the Kelvin Hall, which houses the city's Museum of Transport and is currently home to CR No 123, *Gordon Highlander* and HR No 103. When the River Kelvin overflowed during the weekend of 9-11 December 1994, it flowed down the disused tunnel into Glasgow Central (Low Level), causing much damage. It was some months before the low-level line re-opened.

YOKER (FERRY): This view of the station on 8 June 1962 shows 2-6-4T No 42199 arriving with a Balloch service, having travelled via Glasgow Central (Low Level). The train is crossing over the Rothesay Dock Branch, with Green Road Level Crossing signal box on the left and the power station on the right. *W. S. Sellar*

The 'present' picture has been taken from a lower level because the footbridge from which the other was taken, although still standing, is blocked off as it is unsafe to use. The remains of the station platform facing are just visible in the top left of the picture and the plate girder bridge is still intact, but all evidence of the power station has gone. The four tracks of the branch (the left pair were North British and the right Caledonian) have been reduced to a single line. The branch joins the main line at Yoker Depot, situated midway between Yoker and Garscadden stations. No longer do double-headed 'WD' 2-8-0s pound up the grade from Rothesay Dock with heavy trains of imported iron ore bound for the Lanarkshire steelworks, neither is Lanarkshire coal taken to the docks for export. With virtually no traffic the signal box no longer exists for the crossing.

KILBOWIE: Fairburn 2-6-4T No 42244 leaves the former Caledonian Railway station at Kilbowie with a Glasgow Central (Low Level) to Balloch train on 2 September 1959. With the building of the giant Singer factory adjoining the station and John Brown's shipyard half a mile away, Kilbowie was an extremely busy station in the morning and evening as workers arrived and departed. Within a mile there were no fewer than five stations serving the area: Singer, Kilbowie, Clydebank Central, Clydebank East and Clydebank Riverside. *W. S. Sellar*

With the closure of the Caledonian line in 1964 the track was lifted and the station demolished. Today the area has been landscaped and forms the edge of the car park of Dumbarton East Council Offices. The factory on the right of the 'past' picture still survives but is now hidden by the tree growth.

CLYDEBANK EAST was the terminus of the Glasgow, Yoker & Clydebank Railway (GYC), and opened on 1 December 1882. The GYC branch was opened to convey workers to the re-located J. &. G Thomson Shipyard, which was previously sited in Govan. Thomson's became John Brown's and this famous yard, together with the huge Singer complex, turned Clydebank into a major industrial town. The GYC was subsequently swallowed up by the North British Railway on 15 July 1897. On 2 September 1959 'V1' 2-6-2T No 67664 stands at the station buffer stops. The station was used by local trains and also by excursions to destinations in both Scotland and England before it closed on 14 September of that year. *W. S. Sellar*

The location on 30 January 1997 sees the site occupied by a school and its playing field. The station was joined to the main line by a short spur and the main line can be seen on the extreme left of both pictures. Also the church spire adjacent to the bunker of the 'V1' is still visible today.

HYNDLAND STABLING POINT: 'V3' 2-6-2T No 67627 stands at the stabling point adjacent to the 'old' Hyndland station on 16 January 1960. With Hyndland station being a terminus, there was also a turntable as well as the water tower seen in the picture. The mineral wagons were there to take the ash from locos whose fires had been cleaned out at the stabling point. *W. A. C. Smith*

On 30 January 1997 it can be seen that the site is now a football pitch. The trees are taller and new flats have been built in the space visible in the 'past' picture.

HYNDLAND: The 'old' station is seen on 30 April 1960 with 'V3' 2-6-2T No 67675 accelerating away; it comprised of a long island platform that was used mainly for local services. To the left is the newly opened maintenance depot for the electric units that were introduced on 5 November 1960, which was the date that the last passenger trains used the station. The depot was built on the station's former carriage sidings and it survived until June 1987 when Yoker depot took over. *W. S. Sellar*

The track was lifted in 1988, and on 30 January 1997 there is no sign of the railway's existence, only blocks of luxury flats. The picture has been taken slightly to the left to avoid the tree growth along the retaining wall. However, the church in Hyndland Road remains the linking feature.

HYNDLAND (NEW): The 'new' station opened with the electrification of the Glasgow North Side Suburban services on 5 November 1960 but, following problems with the electrical equipment, steam operation was restored on 19 December 1960. It was ten months later that the electric trains finally took over. During this period Standard Class '4' 2-6-0 No 76093 is seen with an eastbound train on 24 April 1961. *W. S. Sellar*

On 30 January 1997 unit No 320305 is pictured at the station. The platform buildings and footbridge remain as they were, but there have been a number of changes such as the loop being wired and the platform surface being block-paved. The biggest change is the mass of Gartnavel Hospital on the right-hand side.

DRUMCHAPEL: 'V3' 2-6-2T No 67619 enters Drumchapel station with a train for Glasgow Queen Street (Low Level) on 8 March 1958. The station was opened in 1890 to serve the village of that name – few would have envisaged that the small village on the north side of Glasgow would grow into the vast housing scheme it is today. *W. S. Sellar*

At Drumchapel on 30 January 1997 the footbridge is no longer in view, having been moved further east along the platform. The house to the right of the picture remains, as does the housing estate above the rear of the train. The poles and wires of the electrification now dominate the scene as electric multiple unit (EMU) No 302311 arrives with the 12.14 Dalmuir to Motherwell service.

DALREOCH: The Balloch and Helensburgh lines part company at the west end of Dalreoch station. On 2 June 1956 a 'V3' 2-6-2T is seen at Dalreoch Junction with the 5.55pm Bridgeton Central to Helensburgh train. The line to Balloch can be seen diverging on the left behind the signal box. *W. A. C. Smith*

What a clutter at the same location on 14 September 1996, as EMU No 320308 approaches the station from Helensburgh! The electrification masts and wires dominate the scene, but the junction itself remains basically unaltered. The sidings and goods yard have gone, the latter now serving as the station car park, but despite the amount of redevelopment the location is still recognisable.

CRAIGENDORAN JUNCTION: 'V1' 2-6-2T No 67622 approaches the junction on 8 March 1958 with a train for Helensburgh. On the left are coaches stored in Ardmore sidings for summer use. *W. S. Sellar*

On 14 September 1996 EMU No 320302 approaches on a Helensburgh service. The relay room for the West Highland signalling is on the left. The line is now single track with all trace of the carriage sidings long gone.

HELENSBURGH CENTRAL: On 8 March 1958 'V3' 2-6-2T No 67619 is waiting to depart with a train for Airdrie. The generous station layout of two island platforms and large roof structures can be clearly seen. To the right of the picture is the goods yard and the motive power depot. *W. S. Sellar*

The 'present' picture sees a Class 320 unit departing with an eastbound train. The picture was taken from the footbridge seen in the previous picture, because the fence and other building developments prevented access to the 'past' location. The steelwork of the impressive station roof survives but is devoid of glass, largely as a result of serious storms some years earlier. There are only three platform faces now in use, the left-hand track having been removed. There is currently a move to relocate the station to the east of the present site in order to build a shopping complex where the station now stands. No doubt the move will be resisted by the townspeople who enjoy the central location of their station.

HELENSBURGH MOTIVE POWER DEPOT (65H) was a two-road affair situated alongside the station and goods yard, and seen here on 26 March 1960. It had an allocation of about a dozen locomotives at this time, mostly 'V1' and 'V3' 2-6-2Ts for the suburban services. At one time it was a sub-shed of Parkhead (65C) and a number of locomotives allocated to Helensburgh at this time were in fact on loan from Parkhead. The shed was due to close in November 1960 following the electrification of the Glasgow North Side Suburban services, but in fact did not close until December 1962. The delay was due to problems with the electric services, which, for a time, led to re-instatement of steam-hauled trains until they were resolved. *W. S. Sellar*

The site of the MPD is now occupied by a medical centre and, beyond that, a supermarket. The stone wall on the right-hand side of the picture survives on 14 September 1996, as does the tower in the background.

West Highland line: Craigendoran to Fort William

The mere mention of the West Highland Line is enough to bring a smile to the face of any railway enthusiast. The line from Craigendoran Junction to Fort William opened in 1894 and its 140 miles represents one of the great railway journeys in the world. The Extension to Mallaig opened to traffic some seven years later in 1901.

With the arrival of the railway in Fort William the West Highlands were opened up to tourist traffic. However, this increase in passengers lasted only during the summer months; during the winter passenger numbers were light, but in such a sparsely populated area they were never going to be substantial. Local services were limited to the southern half of the line, typically from Glasgow to Garelochhead, Arrochar & Tarbet or Crianlarich.

The opening of the Mallaig Extension saw an increase in freight traffic as fish landed at the port was moved by rail, but, all in all, levels of freight were still relatively low. The Second World War saw a huge increase in traffic to serve the naval bases at Faslane (near Shandon) and at Corpach on the Extension.

After the war there was the inevitable downturn in traffic, but the line survived the Beeching Report in 1963, thanks mainly to the freight.

Dieselisation and radio signalling (RETB) have reduced costs significantly and the line is now open 24 hours a day. The introduction of a summer steam-hauled service in 1984 gave the Extension a boost and this has run every year since, bringing substantial revenue to both the railway and the town of Fort William. In 1995 the steam operation was taken over by the West Coast Railway Company, who are based at Carnforth in Lancashire.

As for the future, with more improvements being made to the Fort William-Mallaig road, the Extension is possibly the most vulnerable stretch of the line, but the traffic figures in recent years, thanks in no small part to the steam service, have been good, and with freight continuing to use the Glasgow to Fort William section it is hoped that the whole of the line will survive for many years to come. With some real marketing of the line both summer and winter traffic could show a substantial increase. When the Fort William to London sleeper service was threatened in 1995, the publicity surrounding its proposed withdrawal generated a huge increase in patronage.

May the sound of trains continue to echo across Rannoch Moor! Their intrusion is barely noticed by the deer who frequent this wild, yet beautiful, place. The railway brings both tourist and local travellers together on what is *the* Great Railway Journey in the United Kingdom.

CRAIGENDORAN (1): 'J37' 0-6-0 No 64580 is seen in charge of an Arrochar-bound train at the West Highland Line platform on 13 August 1960; it is deputising for the 'C15' tank locomotive that usually operated the service. Because of the change of motive power the train is being hauled in the conventional way and is not operating on the push-pull basis employed when powered by a 'C15'. The masts and wires of the North Clydeside electrification can be seen in the foreground platform. *W. S. Sellar*

On 14 September 1996 a 'Sprinter' is working the West Highland line service, and is on the far track as the line has been singled with no platform face. The retaining wall of the Helensburgh line platform remains, but the station lighting and the overhead line supports have been updated. The Helensburgh line has also been singled and the whole station is very run down.

CRAIGENDORAN (2): Standing on the West Highland island platform looking west, there is much activity to be seen on 8 March 1958. On the right is 'C15' 4-4-2T No 67460 with a West Highland line train, while on the left is 'V3' 2-6-2T No 67667 with a train from Helensburgh. Beyond the 'V3' can be seen the lines that ran on to the pier, with the pier itself visible above the loco. Craigendoran Station (West Highland) marked the start of the West Highland line, and opened on 7 August 1894. It closed on 14 June 1964. *W. S. Sellar*

It is a very different picture at the same location on 14 September 1996. The left-hand track and the West Highland platforms and buildings have long been demolished; West Highland trains no longer stop here, the first station being Helensburgh Upper. The magnificent footbridge over the Helensburgh Central lines has been replaced by a much simpler structure, and the pier platform and awning is no more. The pier is no longer rail connected and is in a poor state of repair.

SHANDON: On 1 September 1956 'K2' 2-6-0 No 61776 leaves the island platform with the 3.00pm Glasgow (Queen Street) to Ardlui train. This service only ran on summer Saturdays and a year or two later was extended to Crianlarich. The station was on the hillside high above Faslane Naval Base on Gare Loch, and on 14 October 1895 was the scene of a potentially serious accident involving the 4.20pm Fort William to Glasgow train. The evening was very wild with torrential rain and strong winds, and as the train ran into the station John Crawford, the signalman, did not see it coming and moved the points under it. He then witnessed a horrific spectacle as the two locos and the leading coach ran round the right-hand side of the island platform, the second coach ran on to the platform and overturned, while the remainder of the train ran round the left-hand side. Thankfully only one passenger required hospital treatment, but it could have been so much worse. The station closed on 14 June 1964.
W. A. C. Smith

By 14 September 1996 all trace of the station has gone, although the roof of the adjacent station house is just visible through the bushes on the right. The line is just a single track with no passing loops and very overgrown.

GARELOCHHEAD (1): Class 'C15' 4-4-2T No 67474 is at the south end of the station on 21 March 1959, working the push-pull service between Craigendoran and Arrochar & Tarbet. The station is in good order, with well-kept gardens and, at the top of the pathway leading to the platform, an arch formed of two trees. *W. S. Sellar*

On 12 September 1996 'Sprinter' No 156447 is working the 19.07 service to Oban and Mallaig – the train will divide at Crianlarich. The chimneys of the station building have been removed and the building re-roofed, and although the windows are boarded up and the building is not open to passengers, it is in good decorative order. New lamp standards dominate the scene, but the tree arch still survives. Indeed, apart from the motive power there has been very little dramatic change.

GARELOCHHEAD (2): The 3.00pm Saturdays only Glasgow (Queen Street) to Crianlarich service stands at the north end of the station on 14 June 1958 headed by 'D34' 4-4-0 No 62496 *Glen Loy*. A 'D34' had been requested by the Stephenson Locomotive Society for this train and this was arranged for the Society by Mr James Ness, the Scottish Region General Manager at the time. *W. S. Sellar*

The 12 September 1996 view shows the windows of the station buildings boarded up and the platform festooned with modern lamp standards. The sidings to the west side remain but are overgrown, while the spur to the loading dock has been removed.

ARROCHAR & TARBET: Class 'C15' 4-4-2T No 67474 stands at the station with the push-pull service to Craigendoran. The date is 21 March 1959 and this loco, together with sister loco No 67460, both allocated to Eastfield MPD (65A), were used exclusively on this train. The basic push-pull service was four trains each way per day, but they were never well used, probably because of the distance of the stations from the villages they served. The 'C15' and its coaches were stabled overnight in a siding alongside the station. The loco remained in steam all night, a fireman being dispatched from Helensburgh for this duty, which was not particularly arduous; rumour has it that many an hour was spent dozing in the coaches between checking the fire! A diesel railbus later replaced steam, but this did not prevent the service from being withdrawn on 14 June 1964. *W. S. Sellar*

By 12 September 1996 a new waiting room building has appeared in the foreground, preventing an exact repeat of the 'past' picture. The chimneys on the main building have been rebuilt and the windows boarded up, while trees and bushes seem to be closing in on the track.

ARDLUI: At the north end of the station on 10 May 1962 are preserved CR No 123 and NBR No 256 *Glen Douglas* about to depart with an SLS special from Dundee to Oban. Over the years Ardlui has been one of the least used of the West Highland stations – in 1930 only 887 tickets were issued, bringing in a revenue of just £161! *W. S. Sellar*

Over 30 years later, on 12 September 1996, there has been very little change. The trackwork is the same, but the semaphore signal and the main station building have gone. New lamps now illuminate the platform, which is becoming hemmed in by trees and bushes to the west.

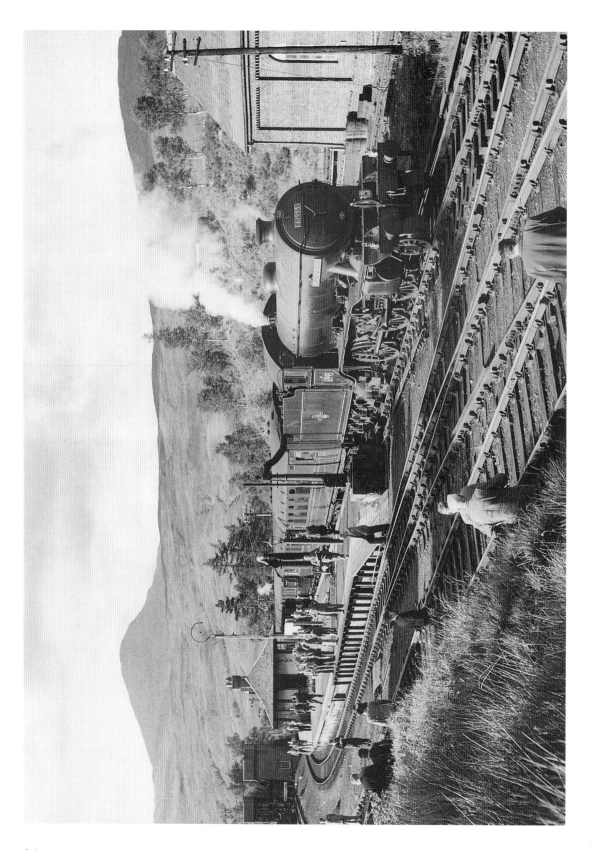

94

CRIANLARICH UPPER: Class 'K4' 2-6-0 No 61995 *Cameron of Locheil* is taking water at the south end of the station on 18 June 1960; the train is 'The White Cockade' excursion from Fort William to Glasgow. The building visible on the right is the old loco shed; one of its last visitors was 'D11' 4-4-0 No 62688 *Ellen Douglas*, which, in ex-works condition, was stored at Crianlarich for several months before being towed back to Glasgow to be scrapped. *Gavin W. Morrison*

On 28 August 1996 combined Fort William and Oban trains depart as a single service for Glasgow (Queen Street). The shed building remains in use as an engineers' depot, but modern platform lighting has replaced the gas lamps of old. The station buildings nearest the camera are modern, as the originals were destroyed by fire. However, at the far end of the platform the earlier buildings still stand. Crianlarich is known as 'The Gateway to the Highlands' and the older buildings house a privately run tea-room that provides a haven for rail travellers and walkers alike.

95

CRIANLARICH CHORD LINE: The chord line opened on 20 December 1897 to link the West Highland Railway's Crianlarich Upper station and the Callander & Oban line at Crianlarich West Junction (see pages 46-7). On 27 August 1965 English Electric Type 1 No D8101 approaches Crianlarich Upper with an Oban to Glasgow freight. The picture presents a rather untidy scene with the telegraph poles and the trackside bushes thick with the leaves of high summer. The one surprising feature is the absence of road traffic. *Noel Machell*

With the passing of years the vegetation has grown up substantially; it was therefore not possible to achieve exactly the same viewpoint, so a lower one had to be used. The road signs have all changed and the bridge has been rebuilt. The old garage in the 'past' picture has gone, but the white buildings still exist, although hidden by the 'Sprinter'. The unit is No 156496 on an Oban to Glasgow (Queen Street) service on 25 August 1996, and the A82 is now much busier.

UPPER TYNDRUM (1): A dramatic sky forms the backdrop as a double-headed morning Glasgow to Fort William train arrives. The combination of a Standard Class '5' (No 73078) and a Stanier Class '5' was quite common on the West Highland Line in May 1961. *Michael Mensing*

At the same spot on 12 September 1996 the semaphore signal has been removed with the introduction of RETB signalling on the line. Otherwise, apart from the points being operated by a ground frame, there are remarkably few changes.

UPPER TYNDRUM (2): Stanier Class '5' 4-6-0 No 44957 stands in the station on a permanent way train on 19 May 1960. The station buildings are of the standard West Highland Railway architecture and look well kept. *Michael Mensing*

This idyllic spot has changed little over the years. But for the boarded-up buildings, taller trees and a white platform edge warning line, by 12 September 1996 the scene remains as it was.

BRIDGE OF ORCHY: The 9.19am Fort William to Glasgow (Queen Street) departs from Bridge of Orchy station on a wet and miserable 23 August 1983. The loco is No 37112, one of many Class 37s to work over the line. *Roger Siviter*

The 'present' picture, taken on 16 September 1996, was taken from a higher viewpoint in order to clear the lineside vegetation. Gone are the semaphore signals, which are not needed with RETB signalling, and the points are spring-loaded, as they are at all the West Highland passing places. There have been very few other changes over the years. Opposite this location on the west side of the line there is a mound that offers photographers an excellent vantage point for southbound trains, and it is always crowded when there is a southbound steam special bringing a loco back from the summer season at Fort William.

LOCH TREIGSIDE: The line runs along the eastern side of Loch Treig, and some 3 miles south of Tulloch station it runs through Fersit tunnel (140 yards). On 16 July 1965 BRC&W Type 2 No D5364 is approaching the tunnel with the 5.45pm Fort William to Glasgow (Queen Street) train. The line is on a steep climb all the way to Corrour summit, but the loch is always visible from the train, giving some spectacular views. *Michael Mensing*

Apart from the tree growth the scene on 30 June 1995 shows little change, except that the traction is a modern 'Sprinter' unit. This stretch of line is not the original; the Lochaber Power Scheme raised the level of Loch Treig by over 30 feet and the line at the north end of the loch was submerged. A diversion was built, including the tunnel, and during construction of the Power Scheme a temporary station was built at Fersit.

TULLOCH: The 5.10pm Fort William to Glasgow (Queen Street) is seen 1 mile to the west of Tulloch and about to pass under the road to the hamlet of Fersit on the sunny evening of the same day, 16 July 1965. The motive power of English Electric Bo-Bo diesel-electrics Nos D8088 and D8084 is slightly unusual; the Class were more often seen on freight duties than passenger workings. *Michael Mensing*

By 28 June 1995 the scene has changed beyond recognition. The background hills are now forested and the track is hemmed in by bushes. No 37428 *David Lloyd George* heads south with empty sleeping coaches for servicing at Glasgow Polmadie depot.

ROY BRIDGE: BRC&W/Sulzer No D5355 arrives at the station with the 6.00am Glasgow (Queen Street) to Mallaig train on 14 July 1965. Roy Bridge (like Spean Bridge and Tulloch) was one of the few stations on the West Highland Line that did not have an island platform. The picture shows that the passing loop has already been removed, leaving just a single platform face in use. *Michael Mensing*

The view of the same location on 30 June 1995 shows that all the station buildings have gone, with the up platform completely overgrown. The background road overbridge remains, and it is from there that locomotives of southbound steam specials take water using a hydrant in the road. 'Sprinter' No 156449 forms a Glasgow to Mallaig train.

SPEAN BRIDGE: No D5368 arrives at the station with a Fort William to Glasgow service on 6 July 1965. The train originated as the 7.48am from Mallaig. *Michael Mensing*

The 'present' picture, taken on 28 June 1995, shows 'Sprinter' No 156453 arriving with the 12.42 service from Glasgow (Queen Street). The old station lighting has given way to an efficient but rather ugly modern-day equivalent. The engineers' siding behind the signal box is still in use, and a large pile of ballast can be seen. The signal box itself is intact but in use as a greenhouse for the station plants. Unlike some of the other buildings on West Highland stations, that at Spean Bridge is in superb condition and is leased from the railway by an enterprising young English couple, Richard and Helen Bunny, who have converted it into a fine restaurant. Well worth a visit!

ALCAN SIDING, FORT WILLIAM: Stanier 'Black Five' 4-6-0 No 44968 gets into her stride 1 mile out from Fort William en route to Glasgow with the 7.40am from Mallaig. The weather on 25 May 1961 is a typically gloomy West Highland day. Despite the fact that it is early summer, the loco is still fitted with a snowplough, ready for the winter ahead. The siding beyond the locomotive leads into the Alcan aluminium smelting plant, the major industry in Fort William. *Michael Mensing*

On 29 June 1995 the siding is still in daily use for receiving raw materials and dispatching finished aluminium ingots. 'Sprinter' No 156445 passes with the 17.40 Fort William to Glasgow service. Low Hill forms the distinctive backdrop to the scene, and while the poles and wires have gone, the semaphore signals remain, operated by Fort William Junction signal box. Meanwhile the vegetation encroaches nearer to the track.

MALLAIG JUNCTION, FORT WILLIAM (1): The view from the A82 trunk road bridge on 7 March 1962 sees the classic combination of Standard '5' 4-6-0 No 73105 piloting Stanier '5' 4-6-0 No 44974 away from Fort William on the 7.40am from Mallaig to Glasgow (Queen Street). The signal box at Mallaig Junction can be seen at the rear of the train, with an incoming freight from the Mallaig direction to the right of the box. *Michael Mensing*

The same location on 27 June 1995 sees 'Sprinter' No 156431 approaching the A82 bridge with the 17.40 service to Glasgow. Fort William Junction (as it is now called) can be seen in the right background, with the roof of the signal box just visible. As is usual nowadays, bushes dominate the landscape, which is now devoid of the pole route and also the factory chimney visible in the earlier picture.

MALLAIG JUNCTION (2): On 22 May 1961 Class 'J36' 0-6-0 No 65300 coasts away from the junction towards Fort William with a short train of alumina wagons from the nearby British Aluminium works. The spare land to the left of the picture became an oil terminal siding. *Michael Mensing*

Thirty-four years later the rail-borne oil traffic has been and gone. The sidings remain in situ, however, and can just be seen through the foliage; hopefully they may again fulfil their purpose. In the meantime the storage depot on the right-hand side is in use, and one of the storage tanks can be seen. 'Sprinter' No 156495 passes on 29 June 1995 with the 16.10 from Mallaig. The semaphore junction signal and the telegraph pole still remain.

MALLAIG JUNCTION (3): Stanier Class '5s' were reliable performers for many years over the Fort William to Glasgow section of the line, and this picture shows No 44972 heading south from Fort William on 26 May 1961 with the train that originally departed Mallaig at 7.40am. There are some oil tank wagons in the siding beyond the train, and under the bridge can be seen the junction, with the Mallaig line diverging to the left. At this date the line was overlooked by some very tall telegraph poles. *Michael Mensing*

Because of the verdant foliage, the 27 June 1995 shot was taken from a lower vantage point and depicts 'Sprinter' No 156436 approaching with the 12.42 from Glasgow (Queen Street). It is passing the disused oil terminal siding referred to in the previous caption.

FORT WILLIAM (1): Ex-NBR 'J36' 0-6-0 No 65313 is seen with the observation coach that it has just removed from the 5.42pm from Mallaig on 20 May 1961. The signal box and bracket signal can be seen to the rear of the coach. This view illustrates just how cramped was the approach to the 'old' station, which made shunting operations extremely difficult. In the right foreground is the footpath that ran between the railway and the sea, and as can be seen it offered an excellent vantage point for photography. *Michael Mensing*

Today the station throat is a large car park with a bypass road to the right beyond the fence. The dormer windows on the distant buildings offer the only link with the 'past' picture.

FORT WILLIAM (2): At the 'old' Fort William station on 1 January 1960 is 'K2' 2-6-0 No 61784 at the head of a train for Mallaig. *W. S. Sellar*

By 29 June 1995 there is no trace of the railway; instead the bypass and car park dominate the scene. With the re-siting of the station half a mile to the east, the old buildings and trackwork were quickly erased from the scene. The only links with the 'past' picture are the church bell-tower and the domed tower of the 'Station Bar'.

FORT WILLIAM (3): 'K1' 2-6-0 No 62034 has arrived at the 'old' station with the 1.00pm from Mallaig on 26 May 1961, and has uncoupled from the stock. Meanwhile 'Black Five' 4-6-0 No 44975 has coupled to the other end and is about to take the train on to Glasgow. This would then release the 'K1' to reverse down to the motive power depot. When the old station closed in June 1975, the original buildings and trackwork were removed within one week of the 'new' station opening on the 13th of that month. *Michael Mensing*
   As can be seen, today rail has given way to road; the fencing has been replaced and the sea-wall re-faced.

FORT WILLIAM MOTIVE POWER DEPOT (1): Midland '4F' 0-6-0 No 44255 stands in the shed yard in 1961 – note the covered tender to keep out the worst of the elements. The depot was coded 63D from 1949 to 1955, 65J from 1955 to 1960, and 63B from 1960 until closure in 1962. It will always be remembered for its large allocation of 'K2' 2-6-0s in the 1950s, and also the 'K1' and 'K4' Classes that were common on the West Highland line. *Michael Mensing*

In the present-day scene on 29 June 1995 only the hill on the far side of Loch Linnhe confirms the location. The shed buildings and yard are long gone and the site is part of the car park for the Safeway supermarket.

FORT WILLIAM MOTIVE POWER DEPOT (2): Looking east on 4 July 1960, we see 'K1/1' 2-6-0 No 61997 *MacCailin Mor* coming on shed. This particular locomotive was a 1945 Thompson two-cylinder rebuild of a 1927 Gresley 'K4' locomotive, and as such was unique. The shed yard is dominated by the mass of Ben Nevis, at 4,406 feet Britain's highest mountain. *S. C. Nash*

On 29 June 1995 there is quite a different structure on the site – a Safeway supermarket with car park. The 'new' station is just out of the picture to the right and beyond the supermarket.

West Highland line: Fort William to Mallaig

MALLAIG JUNCTION: 'K1' 2-6-0 No 62012 nears the end of her journey as she approaches Fort William with the 5.42pm from Mallaig on 24 May 1961. The location is the footbridge over the line near what was then called Mallaig Junction on the outskirts of Fort William. *Michael Mensing*

The semaphore signals still survive at the same location on 27 June 1995. However, it is the right background that shows a dramatic change: where there used to be green fields there is now the Traction Maintenance Depot (TMD). Class 37 No 37410 *Aluminium 100* passes with the return 1995 inaugural 'Jacobite' train, diesel-hauled because of the fire risk posed by steam haulage in the heatwave conditions.

LOCHY BRIDGE: The late evening sun on 3 July 1965 illuminates the bridge over the River Lochy and Lochy Castle as the 6.25pm from Mallaig crosses on its final mile to Fort William. The train is hauled by BRC&W/Sulzer 1,250hp diesel No D5358 with an observation car bringing up the rear. *Michael Mensing*

The present picture, dated 24 June 1996, shows the castle remains undergoing renovation as preserved Stanier 4-6-0 No 44767 coasts across the bridge with the summer 'Jacobite' train. A footbridge has been built on top of the pipeline during the intervening years. The valley of Glen Nevis forms the backdrop.

117

BANAVIE SWING BRIDGE: Crossing the famous swing bridge over the Caledonian Canal at Banavie is 'B1' 4-6-0 No 61342 on a Mallaig train in 1961. Hidden behind the train is the signal box, which not only operated the signalling but also controlled the opening and closing of both the rail and adjacent road swing bridges. *Michael Mensing*

A new signalling centre in traditional style was built alongside the old box in 1987, but was not officially opened until May 1988 and the old box was demolished. The new signalling centre houses the RETB radio signalling that covers all of the West Highland line from Helensburgh Upper to Mallaig, with the exception of the local area controlled by Fort William Junction box. The roof of the new building can be seen above 'Sprinter' No 156492 working the 16.27 from Fort William to Mallaig on 29 June 1995. The old lamp on the end of the bridge has not survived.

CORPACH PAPER MILL: This 1965 view shows the morning Fort William to Mallaig service with BRC&W Type 2 No D5358 in charge. While Ben Nevis dominates the horizon, it is the Wiggins Teape paper mill that fills the picture. It was during the 1960s that railway closures began in earnest, and the West Highland line seemed to be under threat. Just when it seemed that it was doomed, British Railways and Scottish Pulp Developments Ltd entered into an agreement whereby the latter would build a large factory at Corpach and it would be rail-connected. As a result BR agreed to keep the line open for a minimum period of 22 years, and thus the West Highland line was saved. The opening of the Corpach complex produced a substantial impact on rail traffic on the line, with timber being loaded at Crianlarich destined for Corpach. However, the closure of the pulp mill in 1980 lead to a downturn in traffic, but the factory survives to this day and rolls of finished paper still leave by rail on a daily basis. *Michael Mensing*

At the same location on 23 June 1996 much of the factory is hidden by trees. The 'Ben' and the factory look down on 'Sprinter' No 156465 going away from the camera, working the 16.12 Mallaig to Glasgow service.

GLENFINNAN: This 22 August 1983 shot shows Class 37 No 37112 approaching the station with the 06.00 Glasgow to Mallaig train; the 37s were the regular form of motive power for the West Highland line at this time. The signal box is in regular use, working the semaphore signals and controlling access to the engineers' siding, which looks rather weed-grown. *Roger Siviter*

The present-day picture in June 1995 shows No 37403 *Ben Cruachan* approaching with 'The Jacobite'. The semaphore signals have been replaced by RETB signalling, with access to the siding being controlled by a ground frame. The post of the down home signal still stood in 1995, and can be seen above the second coach, while a boarded crossing has been added to provide access to the up platform. The signal box is now part of the Glenfinnan Station Museum project which is chiefly housed in the station building. The 'Glenfinnan Diner', a coach converted into a tea room, sits in the former engineers' siding and is to be joined by a further vehicle, a camping coach.

LOCH DUBH: two miles west of Lochailort D5361 is pictured at the west end of Loch Dubh with the 5.42pm Mallaig to Fort William train on 6 July 1965. Loch Dubh Is sometimes referred to as the Black Loch. *Michael Mensing*

The present-day view on 27 June 1995 sees Class 37 No 37410 *Aluminium 100* in Transrail grey livery. The pole route has gone and the trees and bushes have grown dramatically during the intervening years and now almost obscure the concrete occupation bridge. The Class 37 was deputising for a steam locomotive on 'The Jacobite' service in view of the fire risk in the hot weather.

ARISAIG: On 1 January 1960 a Fort William-bound train is pictured at the station hauled by 'K2' Class No 61784. Apart from the train there is little sign of life, but it is New Year's Day in the Highlands! *W. S. Sellar*

Some 35 years later, the greatest change is in the temperature as the week of 29 June 1995 was a heatwave. The signal box and station are little altered but are no longer in use for their intended purposes. RETB signalling has replaced the semaphores and a ground frame controls access to the engineers' siding. Steam-substitute Class 37 No 37403 *Ben Cruachan*, in green livery, makes an imposing sight in charge of the return 'Jacobite'. Thanks are due to the local permanent way team who acted as look-out while the 'present' picture was taken.

MALLAIG (1) is the most westerly station on the British mainland. In this view, dated 26 May 1961, 'K1' 2-6-0 No 62034 is backing on to the stock that will form the 1.00pm Mallaig to Glasgow service. The station roof can be seen in the right background while the locomotive shed is visible to the left. There is plenty of rolling-stock in evidence, including a row of cattle trucks. *Michael Mensing*

By 29 June 1995 it is a very different picture. The station has been revamped, the trackwork rationalised and the locomotive shed demolished in 1987 to make way for a new road into the town, while units are also being erected on the site to form a small industrial estate. No 37403 *Ben Cruachan* sits at the head of 'The Jacobite' waiting to return to Fort William.

MALLAIG (2): A busy scene on 1 January 1960 with a fish train waiting in the centre road while 'K2' 2-6-0 No 61784 awaits departure with a train for Fort William. The overall station roof is just visible behind the semaphores and the locomotive shed can be seen to the left of the brake-van. *W. S. Sellar*

The changes over the years have been quite dramatic, as shown by this second 'present' view taken on 29 June 1995. All shunting movements are now controlled by a ground frame situated on the right, by the rock outcrop. The new road crosses the site of the old locomotive depot; the 'Welcome to Mallaig' and speed restriction signs can clearly be seen. In stark contrast to earlier years there is no rail-borne freight traffic from or to Mallaig – everything goes by road.

MALLAIG MOTIVE POWER DEPOT: On a dull day in May 1961 'K1' No 62012 is engaged in shunting duties, removing the observation coach from the turntable after it has been turned so that it can be attached to the rear of the train for the return to Fort William. The water tower is to the left of the picture with the stone-built, single-road shed building out of the picture to the right. The depot closed on 18 June 1962 but the shed building was used as a fish store until demolition in 1987. *Michael Mensing*

The June 1995 picture shows that no trace of the depot now exists. The turntable area is being turned into a small industrial estate and a car park for visitors to the town. There is a superb view of the Isle of Skye from here.

Glasgow termini

Buchanan Street

The Caledonian Railway's Buchanan Street station occupied a central location in Glasgow, being situated at the top of West Nile Street. It opened on 1 November 1849 and consisted of only two platforms, the goods station opening two months later. It was anything but a prestigious terminus; the station building was a rather dull single-storey block housing offices and essential facilities and was only a 'temporary' structure, which survived until 1933 when the station was rebuilt.

The platform canopies of the rebuilt station were acquired from the recently closed Ardrossan North, and the station frontage was a steel-framed building finished off with a timber facing. While it was a great improvement on the previous structure it was extremely small, serving just five platforms, but it met its purpose.

Buchanan Street provided services to Oban, Stirling, Perth, Inverness and Aberdeen. In the early 1960s the 3-hour expresses to Aberdeen were introduced, using Gresley 'A4' 'Pacifics' as the motive power.

The goods station, at one time the largest in Scotland, closed on 6 August 1962, with the station itself closing some four years later on 7 November 1966. The site is now occupied by Buchanan Bus Station, Scotrail House and part of the Caledonian University.

BUCHANAN STREET (1): The evening sun illuminates Stanier Class '5' 4-6-0 No 44677 as it stands at the head of the 7.35pm train to Aberdeen on Sunday 23 June 1957. Beyond the train is Buchanan Street Goods Depot, at one time the largest of its kind in Scotland, which closed its doors on 6 August 1962 some four years before the passenger station. The last passenger train ran on 7 November 1966. *Brian Morrison*

The same view looking towards the south-west on 30 March 1997 shows that all the features of the 'past' picture have gone. The Glasgow Caledonian University and its associated car park now occupy the space where the station once stood.

BUCHANAN STREET (2): The departure end of the station sees a pair of North British Type 2 diesels, Nos D6108 and D6135, waiting to leave Platform 1 with the 12.00 noon train to Oban on 13 May 1961. The entrance to the carriage sidings runs behind the locomotives while the cooling tower of Pinkston Power Station dominates the skyline. The signal box to the right controlled movements into and out of the station. Note the fine array of semaphore signals. *Michael Mensing*

On 30 March 1997 one would never know that there had once been a main-line terminus station on the site. The cooling tower and all trace of the railway have gone with the passage of time. The bridge under Dobbies Loan was located where the darker, right-hand part of the retaining wall now stands, and new flats occupy what was once the trackbed.

Queen Street

The Edinburgh & Glasgow Railway opened on 21 February 1842 with Queen Street station as its Glasgow terminus. The original station was a very cramped affair with the platforms extending to the mouth of a tunnel. Cathedral Street ran above the platforms on a metal bridge and was, at one time, over the tunnel entrance. The approach to the tunnel was eventually opened up and some daylight filtered down into the gloom.

From its opening it had four departures per day for Edinburgh, but traffic quickly increased so much that the station was deemed inadequate and was condemned by the Glasgow Magistrates. The North British Railway Company was forced to extend the station by opening up the bottom end of Cowlairs Tunnel in 1877, and this broadened the approaches to the

QUEEN STREET (1): The 2.40pm service to Kirkcaldy, formed of a three-coach Metropolitan Cammell DMU, waits to depart from platform 4 on 27 May 1961. *Michael Mensing*

The present view, recorded on 30 March 1997, shows a couple of 156 Class 'Sprinters' in platform 5; with the exception of the occasional excursion, loco-hauled trains are a thing of the past at Queen Street. The aerial walkway has been removed and there is more glass in the roof than previously.

station and its six platforms. At the same time an overall glass roof was erected. Nine years later, Queen Street Low Level was opened and this took much of the suburban traffic away from the still cramped High Level station. There was also a goods station adjoining the passenger station, but this closed in January 1964, the site now being a car park.

Queen Street quickly expanded in terms of traffic; as well as the Edinburgh services it operated trains to Fife, Perth, Dundee, Aberdeen and, of course, Fort William and Mallaig.

In steam days a departure was always interesting as it required a banker, usually an 'N15' 0-6-2T, to help the train up the 1 in 41 Cowlairs incline. Today the station is extremely busy but locomotive-hauled trains are few and far between, most services being operated by Class 156 or 158 'Sprinters'.

QUEEN STREET (2): The station throat looking down from the Cathedral Street bridge. Apart from the superb semaphore gantry the picture offers an excellent view of the track layout as it existed on 14 May 1960. The train arriving at platform 4 is the 10.10am from Edinburgh Waverley, formed of two three-car Swindon-built 'Cross Country' sets. Spanning the tracks beyond the gantry is the signal box, which afforded the staff an excellent view of the station. *Michael Mensing*
By 30 March 1997 the track has been much rationalised, particularly on the right of the picture. The signal box and gantry have gone, movements being controlled by colour light signals on the platform ends. Much building development is taking place in the area, of which the new bridge is part.

QUEEN STREET (3): Class 'V1' 2-6-2T No 67664 stands at the head of a local train to Kirkintilloch on a sunny 24 April 1961, while to the right 'N15' 0-6-2T No 69181 shunts the goods yard. The cramped conditions of the site are clearly evident as the lines all converge beyond the fine signal gantry and enter the tunnel for the steep climb to Cowlairs. *W. S. Sellar*

The goods yard closed on 6 January 1964 and the site is now a car park and taxi rank. On 30 March 1997 the only linking features are the road bridge, which crosses over the north end of the station, and the girderwork supporting the station roof.

St Enoch

St Enoch station was opened in the heart of the city on 1 May 1876, although the 'official' opening took place on 17 October, by which time trains were running to Kilmarnock, the Ayrshire coast, Dumfries and London St Pancras (via the Settle & Carlisle line). The St Enoch hotel opened for business in 1879, thus completing a very grand station complex. Ownership of the station was assumed by the Glasgow & South Western Railway Company on 29 June 1883, taking over from the City of Glasgow Union Railway.

In its early days around 100 trains a day used St Enoch, but rapid growth increased this to 500 by 1900. This resulted in a further six platforms being added in 1901, bringing the total to 12, and this helped to ease the congestion. The additional platforms added another arched roof to what was already an impressive terminus. It is worth noting that the station was illuminated by electric lighting, the first major public building in Glasgow to use electricity for this purpose.

During the summer months a large number of special trains were laid on to convey Glaswegians in their thousands to the Ayrshire coast, and at times the station was severely stretched with the huge number of passengers using it.

In the 1950s the 'Starlight Specials' were introduced to provide overnight travel to London at a very low fare. Many of these started from St Enoch and on a summer Friday evening it was not unusual to find ten or more 'Starlight' departures from the station, with others starting at Gourock or Clydebank. Competition from the car led to the demise of these trains.

The Glasgow autumn holiday was another hectic time, and the Monday evening of the holiday weekend saw a large number of returning excursions arriving at St Enoch. On this particular day, usually the last Monday of September, the 'Arrivals' board usually displayed

ST ENOCH (1): The two 'past' views are looking north-west from the platform ends on 27 May 1961, when steam was still to the fore. In the first picture, ex-'Caley' '2P' 0-4-4T No 55225 draws the empty stock of the 10.35am from Leeds City out of the station.

The second picture shows 'A3' 4-6-2 No 60082 _Neil Gow_ departing from platform 1 with the 4.00pm to Leeds City. Behind the brick building at the front of the 'A3' can be seen a colour light signal controlling the north-east side of the triangle that led to Saltmarket Junction. _Both Michael Mensing_

The 'present' picture just lacks the railway! The background buildings remain, but where there was once a busy approach to a main-line terminus there is now a car park.

only one station of origin – Blackpool – as train after train arrived from this popular North of England resort.

St Enoch station closed to passengers on 27 June 1966, services being transferred to Central. Parcels traffic continued to use the station for a further year, but on 5 June 1967 that traffic also ceased. For a number of years the station was a large car park, but following the closure of the hotel in 1974 the site was levelled. In its place now stands the St Enoch Centre, a huge glass-fronted shopping complex.

Above ST ENOCH (2): The 2.48pm from Ardrossan approaches the platform ends, also on 27 May 1961. The loco is Stanier Class '5' 4-6-0 No 45362 of Corkerhill shed (67A). Above the loco and first coach is evidence of the 'new Glasgow' – tower blocks of flats under construction. Departures from St Enoch for Ayrshire and the south turned sharp right on leaving the platforms before crossing the Clyde. On the left hand side was St Enoch loco shed, which stood in the triangle of lines between Saltmarket Junction, Clyde Junction and the station itself. The shed closed with the opening of Corkerhill depot, but it continued to be used by permanent way engineers and the red sandstone building remained intact until the station closed. *Michael Mensing*

The present-day picture was taken on 30 March 1997, but looking in a slightly different direction. The flats under construction in the 'past' picture are to the right of this scene, which shows the girder bridge across the centre of the picture forming the eastern chord of the triangle, which is still in use today as a route across the Clyde. The platform ends are now replaced by a car park for the St Enoch Shopping Centre, which stands on the site of the station.

Opposite ST ENOCH (3): A six-coach DMU arrives with the 12.58pm from Stranraer Town on 27 May 1961. After crossing the Clyde the railway ran into the station on a series of arches. *Michael Mensing*

As the arches have all been demolished and the car park is at ground level, the 'present' picture, taken on 30 March 1997, is from a lower vantage point. The capped tower above the Standard Class '4' in the 'past' picture is visible above the word 'MARCH' in the graffiti in the 'present' picture on the brick wall that has been built across the end of the trackbed. The spire still survives as the main linking feature, but with cleaner clock faces.

134

Central

The Caledonian Railway, having been refused access to St Enoch station, planned its own station in Glasgow city centre. Bridge Street station, on the south side of the River Clyde, had been opened on 12 August 1840, and this was rebuilt and re-opened on 12 July 1879 with two through platforms and four bay platforms for local traffic.

In 1873 an Act of Parliament gave the Caledonian Railway permission to bridge the river and open a station on the north bank, right in the heart of the city, hence the name 'Central'. Trains from the south, which had previously used Buchanan Street station, now ran into Central using the new bridge built by William Arrol. The bridge only had four tracks serving eight platforms, and with the huge increase in traffic both the station and the bridge became completely inadequate.

The bridge was subsequently widened and a ninth platform added, but this was of little help, so between 1901 and 1906 the Caledonian Railway built a second bridge over the Clyde and enlarged Central station to 13 platforms; Bridge Street station was closed on 1 March 1905. Central was soon dealing with 500 trains a day and upwards of 25 million passengers a year.

Following the rebuilding of the outside of the station in the early 1900s it has changed little, but inside it is a different story. Following the Glasgow South Side electrification in 1962 and the demise of steam a few years later, the station was given a huge facelift in the 1980s, and today it presents a bright, clean image to the intending traveller. The concourse boasts a fine variety of shops and fast food outlets together with a travel centre and a huge electric Departure/Arrival board.

Opposite CENTRAL (1): On 27 May 1961 'Britannia' Class 4-6-2 No 70050 *Firth of Clyde* stands at the head of the combined 4.30pm to Liverpool and Manchester. The train is in platform 1, which, with platform 2, were always the main-line departure platforms in steam days. *Michael Mensing*

On 6 April 1997 we see the same location but with modern traction. The train is the 12.30 to Euston headed by Mk III DVT No 82120 *Liverpool Chamber of Commerce*. Apart from the overhead wires and the motive power, nothing much has altered over the years, although the stone building looks a lot cleaner than it did in the 1960s and the interior of the station is also much cleaner and brighter than it was all those years ago.

CENTRAL (2): The up 'Caledonian' departs from platform 3 on 21 July 1959 watched by a couple of enthusiasts. The loco is 'Duchess' 'Pacific' No 46240 *City of Coventry* of Camden shed (1B). The 'Caledonian' started running in 1957 but had a short lifespan, being discontinued in the early 1960s owing to increased journey times caused by electrification work south of Crewe. *Gavin W. Morrison*

But for the clutter of electrification there would not be a great deal of change in the location, motive power excepted of course. On 6 April 1997 we see, from left to right, No 86247 departing with the 12.38 to Gatwick, a Mk IV DVT on the 12.45 to King's Cross, and in platform 1 empty coaching stock that has arrived following the departure of the 12.30 to Euston.

CENTRAL (3): BR Standard Class '4' 2-6-4T No 80058 leaves from the west side of the station and crosses the Clyde on 13 May 1961 with the 9.30am to Gourock. *Michael Mensing*

The 'past' picture was taken from another train, and to replicate it would have involved the photographer standing in the middle of the running lines in the station throat! The view taken on 6 April 1997 was therefore taken from the safety of the platform and shows EMU No 303016 departing. The stone bridge pier above the front coach is that adjacent to the fourth/fifth coaches in the 'past' picture. One other similarity – it is another dull day in Glasgow!

CENTRAL (4): 'Duchess' 'Pacific' No 46231 *Duchess of Atholl* rolls over the Clyde with the down 'Royal Scot' on an April day in 1955. The train is crossing the original Clyde bridge, which consisted of five lattice girder spans finished off with iron arches that were really only for decoration. The bridge survived until 1961 when a massive resignalling and track programme rendered it surplus to requirements, all traffic then using the newer bridge, which had been built at the turn of the century. *Gavin W. Morrison*

The same location on 6 April 1997 shows a dramatic change. The old bridge has gone, all tracks are slewed over the newer bridge, colour light signals have replaced the semaphores, and there is the clutter of overhead wires and masts.

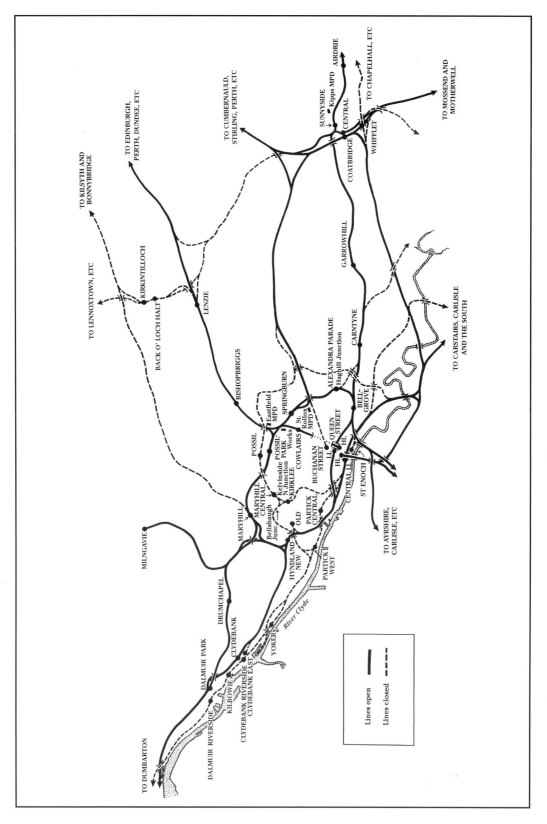

The Glasgow area.

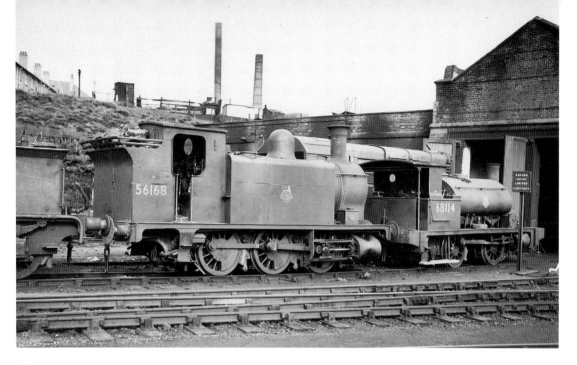

Glasgow, north and east

DAWSHOLM MOTIVE POWER DEPOT (65D): This view of Dawsholm shed, near Maryhill, *circa* 1960 shows 'Caley' Dock Tank No 56168 and North British 'Y9' No 68114. Behind the two steam locos can be seen the outline of a Class 08 diesel shunter. The 'Y9' was allocated to Dawsholm in order to work the Whiteinch Tramway, which ran for most of the length of South Street and was connected to many small sidings with tight curvature, hence the short-wheelbase locomotive. The eight-road shed had an allocation of around 50 locomotives in steam days, the bulk of which were for freight turns. The shed was situated in a very cramped position, the building being tucked in a corner hard against a rock face to the north-east and Kelvindale Road to the south-east. It closed on 3 October 1964 with the majority of the allocation being transferred to either Grangemouth (65F) or Polmadie (66A). *David A. Anderson*

The same view on 30 January 1997 shows that the shed is no more. The area has been cleared and has taken on the appearance of a small park with bushes and trees. Dawsholm's main claim to fame in steam days must surely be the period when the shed was home to the four Scottish preserved locomotives before they were transferred to Parkhead (65C).

BELLSHAUGH JUNCTION: Preserved No 49 *Gordon Highlander* and No 256 *Glen Douglas* head east with an empty coaching stock working. The date is 14 September 1959 and the tall chimney just visible above the tender of No 256 belonged to Kelvindale Paper Mill. *S. C. Nash*

The 'present' picture was taken on 30 January 1997 and shows that all trace of the railway has gone. The high fence in the centre of the picture is where the branch to Dawsholm branched off and crossed the River Kelvin. Just to the left of the high fence is the end of one of the stone bridge abutments. Bellshaugh was part of the Lanarkshire & Dumbartonshire Railway's route from Partick to Possil. This route was in fact three sections, from Partick West to Bellshaugh Junction, then Bellshaugh Junction to Maryhill and from there to Possil. Passenger services were withdrawn on 5 October 1964, with complete closure taking place on 22 February 1966.

MARYHILL CENTRAL: The 4.57pm Clydebank Riverside to Possil train hauled by a Fairburn 2-6-4T has just passed Kelvinside North Junction and is approaching Maryhill Central station on 10 September 1963; the picture was taken from Garrioch Road with the station behind the photographer. This was a 'workers' train to convey some of the thousands who worked at John Brown's Shipyard at Clydebank but who still lived in the Glasgow area. This service and the corresponding morning working were, by this time, the only trains using the west side of the triangle at Partick West. Beyond the last coach the right fork led to Bellshaugh Junction and the left fork to Kirklee. Maryhill station closed on 5 October 1964. *W. A. C. Smith*

On 30 January 1997 only the tenements on the left and the tall building in the right distance link the two pictures. The trackbed is now a walkway and a large Co-op supermarket stands on the site of the station; when it was built space was left in the basement for a single-line platform in case the line was re-opened.

POSSIL: On 12 April 1963 the SLS/BLS 'Easter Rambler' tour is en route to Crianlarich behind preserved CR 4-2-2 No 123. On the left of the picture is the superb waiting room in the form of a small pavilion. The Caledonian Railway's Possil station was opened on 1 February 1897 and closed on 5 October 1964; it was situated just a few hundred yards to the north of the North British's Possilpark station. Note the 'kilted warrior' on the right of the picture, a sight no longer seen on railtours today! *W. S. Sellar*

The site of the station is now occupied by a scrap metal merchant. Because of the scrap and machinery in the way, a higher vantage point had to be adopted on 30 January 1997. The main features are still there, such as the higher land to the right, the distant pylon and, beyond, the housing estate. The area is still rail-served by a new station on the North British line.

ST ROLLOX MOTIVE POWER DEPOT (65B): This view from the bridge on Broomfield Road shows an impressive line-up of locomotives on 12 April 1959, including No 72005 *Clan Macgregor*, No 46228 *Duchess of Rutland* and No 43140. Glasgow Central station was closed for resignalling work this weekend so its main-line trains were being diverted to Buchanan Street with the locos being serviced at St Rollox, which explains the presence of a 'Coronation' 'Pacific'. St Rollox, previously known as Balornock, was a medium-sized depot and in steam days had an allocation of around 70 locos, including a large number of Stanier and (latterly) Standard Class '5' 4-6-0s. At one time all four of the named 'Black Fives' were shedded here, and it also played host to many ex-works locomotives fresh from the nearby loco works of the same name. Consequently many former Caledonian Railway locomotives from sheds in the north of Scotland made appearances from time to time. *Gavin W. Morrison*

The 15 November 1996 picture shows a Class 150 passing the site with the 13.18 Glasgow (Queen Street) to Cumbernauld service. The shed closed to steam in November 1966, and all trace has gone. The area is now a building site, and the railway presence is limited to two running lines, although the background flats still survive, albeit with their chimneys removed.

COWLAIRS BANK: On 12 August 1960 'Black Fives' Nos 44973 and 44975 pound up the 1 in 41 incline, 1 mile out of Queen Street station. They are assisted in the rear by an 'N15' 0-6-2T, which will drop off at the top of the incline at Cowlairs station. The train is the 10.15am Queen Street to Mallaig. The cooling tower and chimneys of Pinkston Power Station dominated the skyline for many years. It supplied electricity to the Glasgow transport system, firstly to the trams, then to the trolleybuses and the underground. Ownership of the power station passed to the South of Scotland Electricity Board in 1958, but it has since been demolished. The line running beyond the train was a siding to the power station and to factories, an oil depot and a distillery in the Port Dundas area; the siding closed in the late 1960s.
Gavin W. Morrison

The legacy of the rush for high-rise flats in the 1960s all but blots out the view of the railway – the track can just be seen at the bottom right of the picture. One sad feature is the amount of vandalism, particularly the throwing of stones at passing trains; it does not pay to concentrate as many people as are in these flats so close to slow-moving trains.

EASTFIELD MOTIVE POWER DEPOT (65A): This general view of the north end of the shed on 12 July 1956 was taken from the viaduct of the Caledonian line, which crossed the site from east to west. The massive coaling plant dominates the scene. To the left of the picture, behind the wagons, was a path that led from the main Bishopbriggs to Springburn road through the Springburn Workmen's Gardens allotments to the shed, used by the writer on many visits to this shed. Eastfield was the largest shed on the North British Railway, opening in September 1904 and closing to steam in 1966. In 1950 it had an allocation of over 150 steam locos, but this had slumped to just six in 1965. Owing to its proximity to Cowlairs Works it was always an interesting shed, hosting many visiting engines either awaiting entry to the works or running-in after overhaul. For many years the shed had large allocations of 'D34' 'Glens', 'D11' 'Directors', 'K2s' and 'K4s', which made it a mecca for visiting enthusiasts from the south. Following dieselisation, Eastfield remained a major depot but its allocation of diesel locos was eventually transferred to Motherwell and the depot closed. *Gavin W. Morrison*

The 8 March 1997 picture had to be taken from a different location as the Caley viaduct, an eight-span plate girder bridge, used for the 'past' picture no longer exists – it ran above the foreground fence. As can be seen, Eastfield shed has been demolished and the track removed, although the dark areas of earth show the former layout. The Queen Street to Edinburgh main line is visible on the extreme right.

BISHOPBRIGGS: 'V1' 2-6-2T No 67601 rolls into the station on 24 April 1961 with the 'Cadder Coach', a train for railwaymen that ran from Queen Street to Cadder Yard. The writer, who for many years lived in Bishopbriggs, used to catch the return working of this train, departing Bishopbriggs at 2.09pm, to journey into Glasgow. On many occasions it comprised an 'N15' 0-6-2T and a single coach. The building to the right is the Crow Tavern, a famous hostelry and funnily enough situated opposite the local police station! *W. S. Sellar*

On 9 March 1997 'Sprinter' No 158720 passes on a Queen Street to Edinburgh service. The Crow Tavern survives, but the down siding has been lifted. New lighting and fencing have been installed on the station.

BACK O' LOCH HALT: Situated half a mile south of Kirkintilloch station on the line to Lenzie, the halt was basically two platforms, one of which had a small waiting shelter. 'B1' 4-6-0 No 61342 of Eastfield shed (65A) is seen leaving with the 6.16pm from Queen Street to Kirkintilloch train. The halt was built to serve a large housing estate on the outskirts of Kirkintilloch, a medium-sized town north-east of Glasgow. The line closed to passengers on 7 September 1964. *W. A. C. Smith*

By 14 September 1996 the site is totally overgrown, although the path to the platform still exists and is just about passable. The station lamps seen in the 'past' picture were mounted on lengths of old rail, and one such length still remains, although the lamp has long gone.

KIRKINTILLOCH: On a drab 24 April 1961 'V1' 2-6-2T No 67664 stands in the station with a southbound train. The station was built on arches with a bridge over a road at the northern end, and was closed to passengers on 7 September 1964. *W. S. Sellar*

The view on 8 March 1997 was taken from a lower level as all evidence of the railway has been swept away. The building with the small tower and spire is now a tandoori restaurant and the building in front of it has had its tall chimney pots removed. The down platform is now the grounds of a nursing home, and the van hire depot is where the second coach of the train stood. A real transformation!

SPRINGBURN: Three-coach EMU No 303081 stands at the buffer stops on 7 June 1964 waiting to form the 4.53pm to Milngavie. The through platforms on the right saw little use, the workers' trains to and from Singer on Clydebank being the regular traffic. The large factory in the background is the Atlas Works of the North British Locomotive Company, whose Hyde Park Works was situated to the right of the station. *Fred Landery*

EMU No 320322 arrives with a train from Milngavie on 8 March 1997. The platform building has been replaced by a 'bus shelter', modern lighting adorns the station, and the Queen Street to Cumbernauld trains now provide a regular service to the through lines platforms. The background has changed completely. The Atlas Works, like the North British Locomotive Company itself, is but a memory; instead there are modern industrial premises and high-rise flats. Those on the left are adjacent to the site of the former St Rollox MPD.

ALEXANDRA PARADE: 'V1' 2-6-2T No 67630 pulls away from the station with the 5.32pm Clydebank East to Springburn train on 5 August 1959. This service only lasted a few more weeks as Clydebank East station closed on 14 September 1959. The station was originally called Alexandra Park, but the name was changed in 1923 to avoid confusion with a station in Manchester. In the background can be seen the two home signals for Haghill Junction, where the left spur led to Carntyne and the right spur to Duke Street and Bellgrove stations; the former connection no longer exists. *W. A. C. Smith*

Owing to the mass of lineside vegetation and a bricked-up bridge an exact replica shot was not possible, but a telephoto shot from the next bridge north, taken on 15 November 1996, shows the salient features. The tenements to the left of the station are clearly visible, but the railway is just a mass of posts, wires and bushes.

GARROWHILL: An Airdrie-bound train enters the station behind a 2-6-2T on 26 March 1960. The wires for the electrification of the system are already in place as two young boys wait for a westbound train. *W. S. Sellar*

On 15 November 1996 there is an entirely different scene as unit No 320305 *Glasgow School of Art* enters with a Drumgelloch (Airdrie) service. The building visible above the steam loco still exists, but the remainder of the industrial buildings on the right have been demolished and the area given over to residential use with blocks of flats. Tower blocks of flats have also been built in the background, and the platform buildings have been replaced by a 'Portakabin'-type structure.

KIPPS MOTIVE POWER DEPOT (65E) was situated in Coatbridge on the North British line to Airdrie, and served an industrial area. The shed consisted of three straight roads and had an allocation of around 50 locos. This view of the western end of the depot in steam days shows 'J36' 0-6-0 No 65214, a 'Y9' 0-4-0ST with wooden tender and a 'J83' 0-6-0T. Prior to the closure of the shed in 1963, the majority of the locos went for scrapping and the building was then used for storage for several months. *David A. Anderson*

On 8 March 1997 all trace of the shed has gone, and the site is just wasteland; the gasholder on the left is the linking feature. The electrified line to Airdrie is behind the photographer.

AIRDRIE (1): 'V3' 2-6-2T No 67660 approaches Airdrie station with a train from Helensburgh. On the extreme right can be seen metal gantry sections awaiting erection for the electrification of the line. The date is 26 March 1960. *W. S. Sellar*

At the same location on 27 July 1996 EMU No 320321 pulls out of the passing loop to draw into the station. The sidings and the second running line have gone, together with all the point rodding and signal wires. The house with the dormer windows still remains but is hidden from view by all the bushes.

AIRDRIE (2): Also on 26 March 1960, but looking east, 'V1' 2-6-2T No 67629 is waiting to depart with a train for Helensburgh via Glasgow Queen Street (Low Level). The overhead gantries are the first signs of the impending electrification of the line and a new signal box is in place. The picture presents an untidy but tranquil scene, very different from weekday mornings and evenings when the platforms were busy with rush-hour traffic. Broomfield, the then home of Airdrie Football Club, was only a short distance from the station, and when Celtic or Rangers were visiting there were up to five extra trains to convey the fans from Glasgow. These extras used to provide a variety of motive power such as 'B1s', 'K2s', 'J36s' and several other classes, as well as the usual 'V1/V3' tanks. *W. S. Sellar*

The present view on 27 July 1996 shows much change. The station consists of a single through platform, to the end of the line at Drumgelloch, and a bay platform. The signal box is out of use as the area comes under the control of the signalling centre at Yoker, and the old station buildings have been replaced with a modern, flat-roofed booking hall. The gable end of Broomknoll Parish Church is still visible to the left of the signal box.

WHIFFLET UPPER: Fairburn 2-6-4T No 42203 is about to leave Whifflet Upper station at Coatbridge with a train for Glasgow Central (Low Level) on 1 September 1959. The line initially ran to Chapelhall but in later years was only used as far as British Steel's Imperial Works. The platform building of Whifflet Lower station can be seen to the bottom right. Passenger services from Upper ceased on 5 October 1964. *W. S. Sellar*

The 'present' scene on 27 July 1996 shows a desolate wasteland where there once was a well-kept station and track. Although overgrown, the platforms are intact on a long bridge. At the far end of the bridge the embankment has been removed and in its place is a large roundabout as part of a road development. The Lower station has been moved half a mile to the south, and the derelict brewery buildings of R. B. Tennant Ltd can be seen to the right of the picture.

INDEX OF LOCATIONS